FOLDOUT:
PROTOTYPE A

EYES ON THE NEWS

The Poynter Institute

For Media Studies

801 Third Street South
St.Petersburg, Florida 33701
Phone: (813) 821-9494
Fax: (813) 821-0583

Eyes on the News book design by Pegie Stark

Cover design and illustration by Nuri Ducassi

Computer graphics and illustrations by George Rorick and Marty Westman, Knight-Ridder/Tribune News Graphics Network

Color photography by Ric Ferro, Florida Fotobanc

Computer assembly and production and editorial coordination by Billie M. Keirstead

Typesetting by Laser Image, St. Petersburg, Florida

Printing by Eva-Tone Printing, Clearwater, Florida

Carmen Miranda artwork by Russ Kramer for Mario Garcia, used with permission

Lobster illustration by David Williams

Drawing of Victorian building, page 3, reprinted from *Bicknell's Victorian Buildings*, Dover Publications, Inc.

"Peanuts" comics, page 58, reprinted with permission from United Feature Syndicate

W July 2-26, 1990 cover, page 59, reprinted with permission from Fairfield Fashion and Merchandising Group, a Capital Cities/ABC, Inc. company

USA Today front pages reprinted with permission from *USA Today*

Dear Abby (Abigail Van Buren) logo, page 47, reprinted with permission from Universal Press Syndicate

Snorkeling photo, page 23, and fashion photos, page 59, reprinted with permission from Ric Ferro, Florida Fotobanc

Pope John Paul II photo, page 46, courtesy of *St. Petersburg Times* and Ric Ferro

New York Times front, page vii, copyright © 1990 by the New York Times Company, reprinted with permission

The following were copied from *Photojournalism* (TIME LIFE books):

　Janis Joplin photo, page 51, reprinted with permission from photographer Joel Snyder

　New York Daily News front, page 52, copyright © 1990 New York News, Inc., reprinted with permission

　NASA moon walk photo, page 52, reprinted with permission from NASA

To the memory of
Nelson Poynter,
whose vision still
colors our craft.

We could hardly contemplate embarking on a study of this magnitude without counting on the assistance of colleagues and friends—academics, editors, designers—all of whom share our desire to explore the many facets of color in newspapers.

At one point during the final stages of production of this book, both of us realized that the project had the feel and fatigue of another doctoral dissertation. Anyone who has ever completed a dissertation learns two things: 1) It can't be done without the encouragement and assistance from generous and candid friends; and 2) for all the work involved, the final product is but an appetizer to one's lifelong involvement with the subject.

Indeed, this study has only intensified our own interest in color; the more we learned, the more we found there is to explore.

To those "generous and candid friends" who paid careful attention to detail and were so willing to help us perfect our work, we are most grateful.

The honor roll begins with our colleagues at The Poynter Institute for Media Studies. On top of the list is our managing director, Bob Haiman, whose faith and support date back to our first color research project in 1985. High among the honored is our dean, Roy Peter Clark, who believes color in the newspaper goes beyond colorful writing; Ed Miller, for his thoughtful solutions to both design and editing problems along the way; Don Fry, who directs our writing programs and took time to scrutinize our findings and play devil's advocate; Billie Keirstead, director of publications, for lending her computer skills and expertise in the production of the book; editorial assistant Lisa Compton for her excellent attention to detail; and Martha Daughtry, our "right hand," who kept us on track throughout the project.

Anyone who takes a close look at the prototype pages used to test our concepts will soon realize what it must have been like to replicate pages with different degrees of colorization (or just black and white) in three different cities across the country. To the management of the *St. Petersburg Times*, the Minneapolis *Star Tribune*, and *The Orange County Register* in Santa Ana, California, our gratitude for volunteering so many talented staffers to help with this project. Specifically, we thank Andy Barnes in St. Petersburg, Chris Anderson in Orange County, and Roger Parkinson in Minneapolis for their unqualified support.

When production actually began, the following staffers answered the call: in St. Petersburg, Neville Green, Mike Foley, Trich Redman, Ron Reason, Anne Hand, Pauline Brockman, and George Sweers; in Minneapolis, Tim Bitney and members of the news and art departments; in Orange County, Bill Dunn, Tom Porter, and numerous editors and artists.

Because the entire project depended upon the use of the EYE-TRAC® Research equipment of Gallup Applied Science of Princeton, New Jersey, we are indebted to its experts, particularly Dr. Sharon Polansky and Sally Gullette.

Other creative support came from Nuri Ducassi, art director of *El Nuevo Herald* in Miami, whose cover design captures the spirit of the study; George Rorick, director of the Knight-Ridder/Tribune News Graphics Network, whose informational graphics translated the results into reader-friendly formats; Nanette Bisher, assistant art director of *U.S. News & World Report*, and Prof. Robert Eagerton of the John Herron School of Art in Indianapolis, who gave us valuable assistance in the editing of the Color Primer chapter.

Both of our families have given us encouragement and support throughout the project. We could not have completed it without their understanding.

Finally, we would like to thank the editors, designers, artists, and academics who took the time to reply to our initial questionnaire about color use in newspapers. We hope their efforts have been compensated by the answers found in this book.

Dr. Mario R. Garcia
Dr. Pegie Stark

ACKNOWLEDGMENTS

The contents of this book surprised the Helvetica out of me.

As I read it, I sat scratching my head as myth after myth about newspaper reading fell by the wayside. By the time I got to the end, I felt a little lost. What kind of force is color in American newspapers? Should anyone still invest that $50 million in those new color presses?

Relax. Spend the dough. We live in a color world, and there's no doubt that color attracts readers to news pages and advertising. But don't stop there. Invest another million in professional development of reporters, editors, artists, and designers. Get them talking about working together to create newspapers that serve readers in their diversity.

For it turns out that using color is a tool, not a rule.

Here are some of the surprising results of the Poynter EYE-TRAC® Research:

■ I knew that photos, especially big ones, help draw readers into pages. But I had always thought that color photos automatically drew more readers. Not so. The content, size, and placement of photos are much more important. Color alone is not the powerful magnet we've always thought it to be.

■ I had always accepted the wisdom that readers begin reading at the top-right corner of the front page, looking for the most important story. (Didn't Ed Arnold teach us that in Deuteronomy?) Forget it. This study suggests that readers will enter the page wherever the most powerful element is—right, left, middle. And depending upon the look of the page, they are willing to follow trails that editors lay for them.

■ Now get this. You know how we've always acted as if individual newspaper pages are discrete units that readers process separately? I think that myth just vanished up the chimney. Readers look at facing pages as single units. Designers should be aware of that. By the way, that means that letting one editor design Page 2 and another do Page 3 may not make sense.

Readers enter a page through the dominant element.

■ Color is still relatively new to American newspapers. There is the perception that readers can't tolerate too much of it, or that they will only accept the most subdued or traditional approaches to color selection. Well, get out your crayons, because it looks as if readers will accept some bold, even outrageous experiments that may be hard to track on your color wheel.

Readers look at facing pages as one unit, not two; what's more, they look at the right-hand page first and then travel to the left.

■ Here's the biggest shocker to me. Maybe because I learned my journalism in St. Petersburg, I've always thought of color in newspapers as this irresistible force. Sure, color attracts attention, but (imagine this next sentence printed in magenta)

COLOR DOES NOT CONTRIBUTE TO OR DETRACT FROM A READER'S ACQUISITION OF VISUAL INFORMATION.

Is that true? Well, almost.

It appears that color is just one of many tools that editors can use to present the news to readers in powerful ways. Color seems not to work independently, but synergistically. That last fancy adverb means that a skilled editor can use color to enhance or intensify the reader's journey across the page. But size, position on the page, page architecture, and content of photo or story are just as important.

The bad news, at least for some editors, is that color is not a magic bullet. You can't quick-fix your way into a livelier paper or a growing number of readers.

The good news, especially for a "word-man" like me who has been suspicious of the color revolution, is that journalistic craft is king. The editor, as part of a collaborative team of journalists, must create a path for readers to follow on the page. What is most important, most interesting, most urgent, most worthy of attention? The editor must use *all* the tools on the workbench to communicate the news of the day: the powerful photo, the punchy headline (in the right typeface and size), the well-crafted cutline, the appealing illustration, the well-told story. Great color is another tool. But using color well requires the exercise of editorial judgment.

Maybe I shouldn't be so surprised after all. We've preached here at The Poynter Institute for a long time the primacy of content and the exercise of craft on behalf of the readers. Some of the most valuable real estate in journalism—the front page of *The New York Times* or *The Wall Street Journal*, or the text of *The New Yorker* magazine—is constructed without color. Those publications can inform readers with integrity (but without color) because they have mastered the other tools of the craft.

But living as we do in a world of color, we recognize its mysterious magnetism. Color creates an aesthetic environment in which readers, especially certain readers, feel comfortable. When used well, color attracts, pleases, and helps inform us. When used for its own sake, color counts for little. When used to enhance and support sound journalistic decisions, color is the powerful tool we've always thought it was.

To use color powerfully, journalists must operate from facts, not just gut-level hunches and shards of conventional stylebook wisdom. That's why The Poynter Institute paid for this research by my colleagues Mario Garcia and Pegie Stark: To help journalists make better decisions in the interests of readers.

Roy Peter Clark
Dean of the Faculty
The Poynter Institute

"For it turns out that using color is a tool, not a rule."

CONTENTS

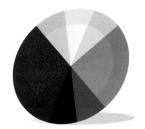

Color Primer/ 19

Reading/ 39

As the pursuit of more colorful newspapers gains momentum around the world, two questions about color continue to haunt editors and publishers:

1. Does color help sell newspapers?

2. Is color here to stay?

The first question is usually asked by a senior editor, often over age 50, who defiantly demands proof: "Can you prove to me that one more copy of a newspaper is sold because of the presence of color?"

My answer? Content sells, but color can help. I know of no case where color—and color alone—has led to increased sales. It's the content of a newspaper, the editor's imaginative approach to articulating and presenting the news, that makes the difference. "Colorful content" is far more important than the "colorization" of the pages.

Nevertheless, color does attract. This is especially true for younger readers, who have become increasingly difficult to convert to the habit of newspaper reading. Of equal importance are the attitudes of advertisers, whose desire for color is well documented. So, although color itself may not sell an extra copy of a particular edition, over time the ability to provide color can make a significant difference in both reader appeal and revenue generation.

The answer to the second question is easier. Yes, color is here to stay in newspapers, just as it is in television and magazines. It's no longer an option; it's an essential ingredient. We have to remind ourselves that only a generation ago color was perceived by some as detracting from a newspaper's "serious" image. But Nelson Poynter, a visionary publisher, saw color in the future of newspapers. By the mid-1970s, the *St. Petersburg Times*, a newspa-

per with a tradition of journalistic excellence, was regularly publishing color on the front page. It wasn't long before the *St. Petersburg Times* became a daily text on the use of color. It learned principles of color use that still apply: Make it functional, use it with restraint but on center stage, and less is best. The *Times* helped create an awareness and acceptance of color in American newspapers, a contribution that should not go unheralded.

By the mid-1980s, readers had come to accept color in newspapers without reservation, as they had years before in television. We must remember that three-quarters of our readers today cannot recall life without television, and most of those video memories are in color. This is a number that can only grow. Highly respected newspapers like *The Washington Post* and

the *Los Angeles Times* followed the lead of countless smaller newspapers and began introducing color into feature sections. By the time its 1989 redesign was completed, the *Los Angeles Times* had taken color all the way to its front page.

A color model for the 1980s was *The Orange County Register* in Santa Ana, California, where editorial innovation was teamed with original and creative uses of color.

INTRODUCTION

1

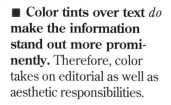

The *Register* was to the 1980s what the *St. Petersburg Times* was to the 1970s. Both newspapers are successful, and most likely they would be without color, but I'm confident the creative use of color attracted and retained readers who might otherwise have drifted away.

The experiments of the 1980s enabled us to study color, analyze how its use could lead to increased readership, and learn more about eye movement around a typical newspaper page. The 1985 Poynter Institute Color Research initiated that process. Assisted by Dr. Robert H. Bohle of Virginia Commonwealth University, I was able to isolate a number of variables that led us to greater understanding of color. From these lessons we could create more interesting and attractive pages, and also train editors and designers how to get the most from their use of color. The 1985 study provided us with a set of guidelines:

■ **Color can guide the reader's eye from top to bottom on the page.** For designers, this means it is better to take one color and organize the page around it than to introduce a variety of clashing colors that create visual disorientation.

■ **Readers prefer color over black and white when presented with a choice.**

■ **Color tints over text *do* make the information stand out more prominently.** Therefore, color takes on editorial as well as aesthetic responsibilities.

■ **The size and placement of a photograph appear to have greater importance than the question of color versus black and white.**

■ **Positioning of color ultimately affects how the eye moves around the page.**

The findings of the 1985 study can be found in *Color in American Newspapers*, a publication available from The Poynter Institute for Media Studies. Although much has been written about color perception in fashion, architecture, film-making, and interior design, little of that applies directly to newspapers. The 1985 study was the first systematic effort to provide data and conclusions that would guide the implementation of color in newspapers.

Indeed, that study changed my own sense of color. I began using it as a design tool of equal rank with typography and page architecture.

"Franz Liszt once described a composition he was writing as needing a little pink here, there sounding too black; overall, he wanted it sky blue."

Designer's Guide to Color

I approached color with less ambiguity, more confidence. I began to see contemporary newspaper design as a symbiotic relationship of three interrelated processes—typography, architecture, and color—converging on the canvas of the page. But the relationship is still unequal. Years, indeed centuries, of research on typography and page architecture have made us confident craftsmen with these tools, but color still perplexes. There simply hasn't been enough research on newspaper color.

Yet, there was a growing interest and need in the industry for information about color. By mid-1988, Dr. Pegie Stark and I drew up plans for a new, more encompassing study using the technology of EYE-TRAC® Research equipment designed by Gallup Applied Science of Princeton, New Jersey.

Our first step was to send a questionnaire to publishers, editors, and designers around the world. The responses sharpened our insights about the kind of research needed. After identifying the variables to be studied, we began to create the prototypes, using the talents of our colleagues at the *St. Petersburg Times,* the *Star Tribune* in Minneapolis, and *The Orange County Register* in California.

The results are the industry's most current data about how readers actually move through the pages of newspapers. This research

will be helpful to publishers committing millions of dollars to color-press technology, editors and designers making page-layout decisions, and academics researching links between page design and reader comprehension.

Before we started the study, we believed that color is a permanent fixture in newspapers and that it helps attract and retain readers. Now we have a better understanding of how and why.

Mario R. Garcia
November 1990

HOW TO READ
THIS BOOK

The Poynter Institute for Media Studies, using the EYE-TRAC® Research technology of Gallup Applied Science, conducted this study to determine how color affects newspaper reading.

In each of the markets for three newspapers—the *St. Petersburg Times*, the Minneapolis *Star Tribune*, and *The Orange County Register* in Santa Ana, California—two prototypes were created, each matching the local newspaper in style and format.

The two prototypes in each city were similar in content and format except for carefully planned variations designed to test the influence of color.

As participants paged through one of the prototypes, their eye movements were tracked by two miniature video cameras attached to an oversized headband. One camera recorded the movements of the reader's pupils; another (the "scene" camera) recorded what the reader was looking at. A computer synthesized the two images and created for the researchers a videotape of the newspaper pages showing the tracks of the eye movements across each page.

Ninety participants were tested. The analysis of their eye movements is the basis of this book.

DEFINITION OF TERMS

Throughout the book we use words and descriptions that require some initial explanation. Here are four concepts crucial to an understanding of the data:

Processing opportunity

Every element in the prototypes represents an opportunity for that element to be looked at, or "processed." Therefore, every headline, photo, cutline, and story is a "processing opportunity."

Processing

An element is "processed" when a reader looks at it. That's all; just looks. To "process" something, the reader's attention stops long enough at an individual element—a cutline, photo, or bit of text—for information to be acquired, or "processed."

Reading

If the reader's eyes move across one or more lines of print from left to right, the material is considered "read."

In-depth reading

When at least half of any text is read, it is considered read "in depth."

To summarize, a single element such as a photograph or the text of a story is a "processing opportunity" for each reader participating in the test. If there are 25 photographs in the prototype, that means there are 25 opportunities to look at, or "process," photographs.

When a reader stops to look at an element, that element is considered "processed." If the reader looks at ("processes") five of the 25 photographs ("processing opportunities"), we conclude that 20% of the photos are processed. This does *not* mean the remaining 80% are not looked at by anybody. It simply means that of all the opportunities by all the participants to see photographs, *on the average* 20% are actually looked at.

Obviously, this definition of "processing" is a low threshold, particularly for long or complex text. How do we determine when a participant actually "reads" something? If a reader's eyes move left to right across one or more lines of text, then the story, headline, or cutline is considered "read."

Because reading one line is still not a high threshold of activity, we use a third category: "in-depth reading." If half the text is "read," we consider it read "in depth."

Three more explanations are in order:

- The results are reported in the *present* tense. This is a simple style decision, but it has some implications. Reporting that "readers enter the front pages at the dominant photo" seems to imply that *all* readers of *all* newspapers do that. The results may sound more universal than we intend. Although some results might be widely applied, it is our mission here to report and analyze the findings of a single research project. Don't be misled by the power of the present tense.

- The results reported are composites of the three test sites, unless otherwise noted. So when we say "participants processed 25% of the text," that is an average of all the participants, even though an accompanying graphic may show a page from a specific city.

- Be aware, too, that tests of prototypes can produce higher numbers than tests of "real" newspapers. Prototypes are smaller and easier to read. There are fewer ads to compete with editorial text, and the package is filled with interesting stories and high-quality artwork. So it would be a mistake to assume that the precise results of all aspects of a prototype test apply to all "real" newspapers. The conclusions may be accurate, but the numbers should be used with caution.

BOOK DESIGN

Foldouts

You can see the two prototypes tested in this study by unfolding the flaps inside the front and back covers: Prototype A appears in the front and Prototype B in the back. Throughout the book we refer to pages in these prototypes. The foldouts will help you see the differences at a glance. For example, look at the front page of Prototype A. Now look at its counterpart in Prototype B. The contents of the two pages are identical, but the color has changed.

Chapter organization

We begin with a brief explanation of how the prototypes were designed, and give a detailed account of the testing itself, including how participants were selected and how the EYE-TRAC® Research equipment works.

Following that is a primer on color. It's not our intention to review all the color research since Sir Isaac Newton got in the business in 1676, but editors and artists should know how the eye works and be aware of some predictable physiological responses to color.

Four chapters present the results of the study:

- **Points of Entry**
- **Reading**
- **Photos & Art**
- **Color in the 90s**

After the findings are reported, a final "discussion" among the authors and various experts on writing, editing, and research attempts to draw conclusions from the data and make connections for the readers of this book. Roy Peter Clark, dean of The Poynter Institute faculty, has the last word with suggestions on how readers might use the information.

A bibliography prepared by Jo Cates, chief librarian at The Poynter Institute, ends the book.

COLOR SURVEY
PROTOTYPES
PARTICIPANT SCREENING

SURVEY

Before creating the prototypes for the EYE-TRAC® Research color study, we asked editors, designers, academics, and art directors to help us determine what issues needed more research.

Here are some of the results of that survey.

Which U.S. newspapers serve as color models for you?

(Ranked by the number of times mentioned.)

1. Orange County Register
2. USA Today
3. St. Petersburg Times
4. Washington Times

Which areas are most worthy of study in terms of eye movement?

1. Impact of color photos
2. Time spent with story
3. Impact of color as an organizational tool
4. Effect of color quality

Which colors would you like to receive more information about?

1. Peach
2. Blue
3. Red
4. Black and white

Which topics are most important for color research?

1. Color preferences of readers vs. editors
2. Color and black-and-white photo mixes
3. Effect of complementary vs. contrasting colors
4. Gray as a "color"

Most newspapers have color "philosophies." They include:

■ Use color to make a statement, not for its own sake.
■ Use a lot of color; use it well.
■ Use color as a news tool.
■ Keep it clean and simple.

OTHER SURVEY RESULTS:

■ People making color decisions generally learn how to use color on the job or at seminars.

■ 87% agree that color sells newspapers.

■ Most rate newspaper color use as average.

■ Most believe color can affect credibility.

■ 83% say they will increase color use in the next five years.

THE TEST SITES

We chose three newspapers to help us conduct our study: the *St. Petersburg Times* in St. Petersburg, Florida; the *Star Tribune* in Minneapolis, Minnesota; and *The Orange County Register* in Santa Ana, California. The newspapers had comparable color printing capabilities and strong reputations for the generous use of quality color.

Furthermore, the three cities were selected to give the study some geographic and ethnic diversity.

THE PROTOTYPES

Our first challenge was to create realistic prototypes in each city. That meant conforming to the formats and styles of the three participating newspapers. This was important, for if we had created a prototype using formats unfamiliar to readers, we might have hindered their customary reading patterns and thereby affected the results of the test. So in each city the local newspaper's daily design format, including typography, grid structure, and design style, were followed carefully.

Two 20-page prototypes were created for the study (see Prototypes A and B on the cover foldouts). Each page tested color questions uncovered in the findings of our initial survey. For example, the photographs on the front page of Prototype A were all in color. There was also a color screen on the digest. Prototype B was identical in content and format, but the photos were in black and white and the color screens were not used. By comparing how readers "read" these pages, we hoped to assess the impact of color vs. black-and-white photos as well as the impact of color screens.

There was no single "color" prototype. The color to be tested was placed throughout both prototypes.

The original prototype was created at the *St. Petersburg Times*. The *Star Tribune* and *The Orange County Register* followed suit, changing the format and style to conform to their local traditions.

Ron Reason, Page One editor at the *Times,* and Trich Redman, art director, selected the contents of the prototypes. Because the

---

THE THREE TEST SITES

Test sites were chosen for their geographic location, size, and population diversity. Newspapers were chosen for their printing similarities and daily color capabilities.

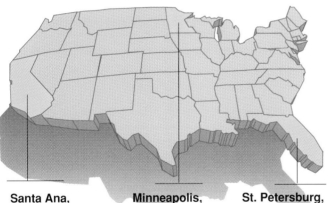

Santa Ana, California	Minneapolis, Minnesota	St. Petersburg, Florida
Orange County Register	**Star Tribune**	**St. Petersburg Times**
Population: 2,304,515 (Orange Cty.)	Population: 1,711,100 (Minn.-St. Paul)	Population: 855,427 (Pinellas Cty.)
Circulation: Daily: 346,439 Sun.: 398,897	Circulation: Daily: 410,226 Sun.: 663,063	Circulation: Daily: 341,363; Sun.: 437,654
Presses: Goss Metroliner	Presses: Goss Headline Offset	Presses: Goss Metroliner
Color scanner: Hell	Color scanner: Kodak-Atex Design Master	Color scanner: Crossfield

Sources: Marketing and research departments at *Orange County Register, Star Tribune, St. Petersburg Times.*

testing would take place over a four-week period, news stories had to be timeless, but not so evergreen that they lacked the urgency associated with news. It was easier to select features that would remain current and interesting over the test period.

Stories, photos, and graphics were transmitted to Minneapolis and Orange County, where local editors and artists adapted the content to local styles and design formats.

Color positioning, choice of color screens, and size of color image were similar in the three test sites.

There were some minor differences in the prototypes from city to city. For example:

■ The lead story in the *Star Tribune*, following that newspaper's custom, appeared at the top of the front page on the left. The *Times* and the *Register* placed the same story top right.

■ Front-page promos or teasers also followed the specific style of the individual newspapers.

■ Because of different page grids and column sizes in each city, some elements varied slightly in size and length. These differences were not considered significant by the researchers.

■ Conforming to style, some of the headlines were worded differently in each city.

■ Store names changed in the advertisements, giving the prototypes a local flavor.

■ The last page of each prototype displayed a local story specific to that market. Each newspaper used a color photo of a local sports figure along with a blue screen over text. In Orange County, the ad was different as well.

PARTICIPANTS

Participants were screened by phone prior to testing and again at the test site to make certain they met two criteria: age and newspaper reading frequency. The researchers wanted participants between ages 25 and 43 who were considered frequent newspaper readers, that is, readers who had read a newspaper on at least four of the last seven days.

The readers actually selected met the criteria. In fact, the participants were unusually "frequent" readers of newspapers. On average they read a daily newspaper more than 6 days a week.

The actual tests used 30 participants at each of the test sites. Of the 90 participants, 42 were female, 48 male. Overall, about 80% of the participants were white, about 20% nonwhite. The Orange County site had the highest ratio of nonwhites.

As a reader looks through the newspaper, two miniature cameras attached to a headband record his eye movements.

THE THREE PROTOTYPES

We chose three newspapers representing diverse markets. The original design was created at the *St. Petersburg Times*. Each paper maintained the integrity of its own individual design, but used the same stories, photos, and illustrations used by the *Times.*

EYE-TRAC® RESEARCH

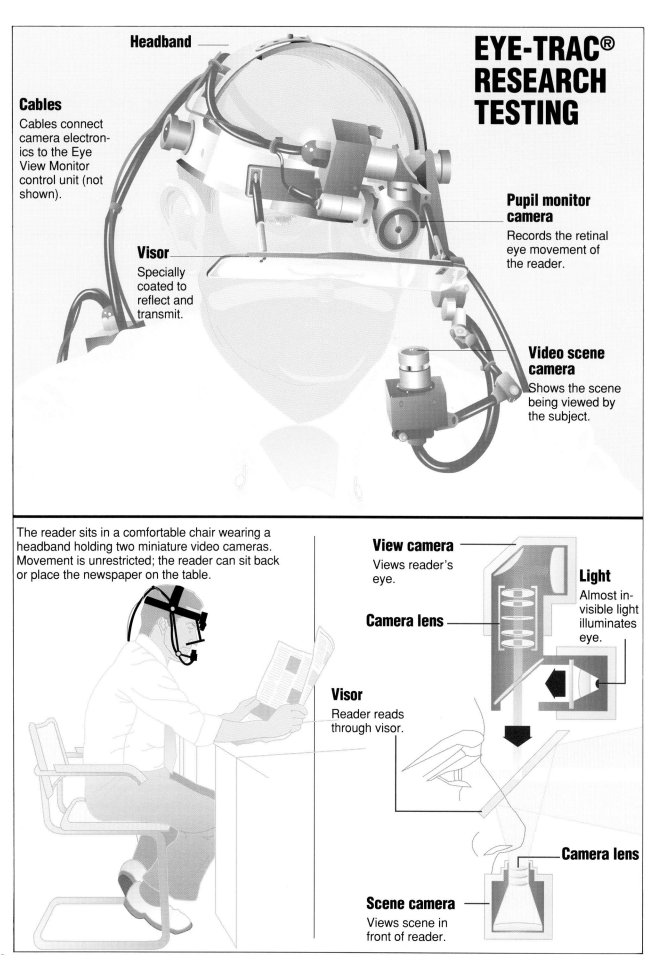

Headband

EYE-TRAC®
RESEARCH
TESTING

Cables
Cables connect camera electronics to the Eye View Monitor control unit (not shown).

Pupil monitor camera
Records the retinal eye movement of the reader.

Visor
Specially coated to reflect and transmit.

Video scene camera
Shows the scene being viewed by the subject.

The reader sits in a comfortable chair wearing a headband holding two miniature video cameras. Movement is unrestricted; the reader can sit back or place the newspaper on the table.

View camera
Views reader's eye.

Light
Almost invisible light illuminates eye.

Camera lens

Visor
Reader reads through visor.

Camera lens

Scene camera
Views scene in front of reader.

HOW THE TESTS WERE DONE

Before the test

An interviewer confirms each participant's age and paper-reading frequency.

The environment

The testing environment is designed for comfort and simplicity. The participant can sit back in a swivel chair to read, or can rest the newspaper on a table.

The testing device

The EYE-TRAC® Research equipment is on a nearby table, attended by an operator. The heart of the system is two miniature television cameras strapped to a headpiece worn like a cap. While the equipment is calibrated, participants read a "real" newspaper (not a prototype).

Recording eye movement

The participants are given either Prototype A or B to read. They never see the other prototype during the test.

There are no time limits. Participants can read as long as they wish. Overall, readers in this study average nearly 17 minutes reading the prototypes.

Despite the headgear, readers are free to move their head and hands as they read. They can use the table or put the newspaper in their laps. While they read, their eye movements are recorded on a videotape.

The exit interview

When the testing is completed, the participants are taken into another room for an exit interview. Exit interviews are discussed in the Reading chapter.

The final videotape

The session produces a videotape of each person looking at the prototype newspaper. This tracking technique records where the reader entered the page and the number of elements—headlines, photos, cutlines, and text—looked at along the path through the page. By seeing how long the eye remains on any one element, the researchers can determine to what degree the material is processed.

The Result

As the reader looks through the paper, the cameras record the journey. A cursor tracks the reader's eye movements, showing each item looked at. The movement is recorded on videotape for analysis.

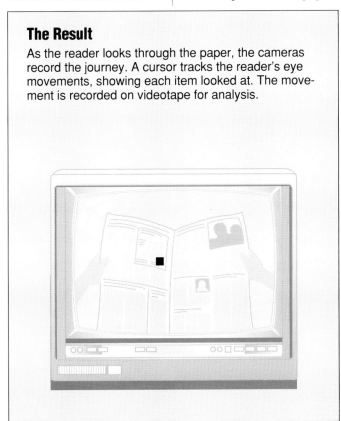

COLOR PRIMER

EARLY COLOR EXPERIMENTS

Sir Isaac Newton performed the first known color experiments in 1676 at Trinity College, Cambridge, England. He outlined his discoveries in *The Opticks*, published in 1704. His work focused on light and visual perception, but during his experiments he discovered that sunlight was actually a composite of colors, each with a different wavelength. He demonstrated this by allowing sunlight to enter his room through a small slit in the wall and placing a prism in the path of the light. The result was a ray revealing all the spectral colors, from red, orange, and yellow to green, blue, dark blue, and violet.

When Newton placed another prism in line with the color spectrum from the first, it recombined the colors to produce white. Thus he discovered additive color.

How light makes color

Sir Isaac Newton discovered that sunlight directed through a prism creates all the colors of the spectrum. Here is how he set up his experiment.

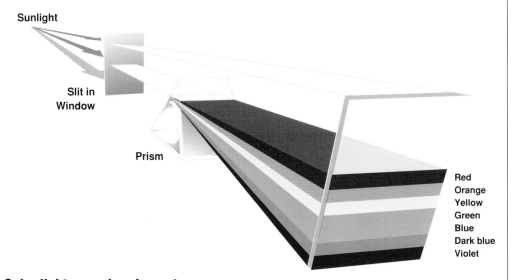

Sunlight

Slit in Window

Prism

Red
Orange
Yellow
Green
Blue
Dark blue
Violet

Color light vs. color pigment

When all the spectral color lights are mixed, they produce white. When all the color pigments are mixed, they produce black.

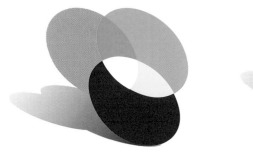

Additive color: Color lights combine to produce white.

Subtractive color: Color pigments combine to produce black.

Source: Johannes Itten, *The Elements of Color*, p. 15

THE COLOR WHEEL

Color wheels display the primary colors—red, yellow, and blue—and all the color combinations based on the primaries.

When working with color, three factors must be considered: hue, saturation, and brightness. Hue is the pure color. Saturation refers to the amount of pigment present, and brightness varies with the amount of black in the mixture.

Complementary colors

Complementary colors are opposite one another on the wheel. For example, the complement of red is green, the complement of yellow is purple.

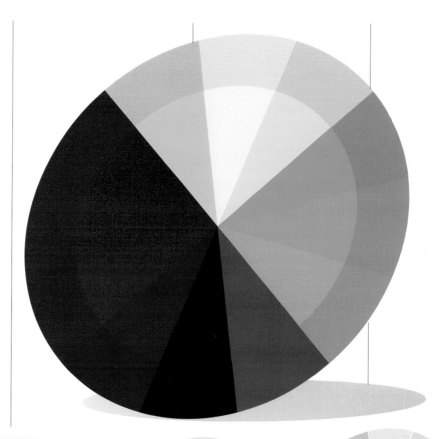

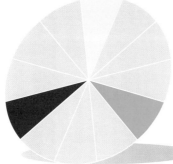

Primary colors
Red, yellow, and blue.

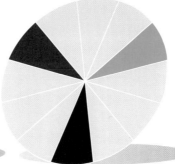

Secondary colors
By mixing two primary colors, we create the secondary colors: orange, green, and purple.

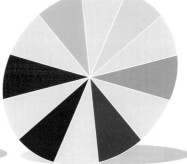

Tertiary colors
By mixing a primary color with a secondary, we create the tertiary colors: red-orange, red-violet, blue-violet, blue-green, and yellow-green.

Colors and wavelengths

Colors are a result of waves of light varying in length. Our eyes can distinguish wavelengths from 400 to 700 millimicrons.* All the spectral colors fall within that range.

* 1 millimicron = 1/1,000,000 mm.

400   700

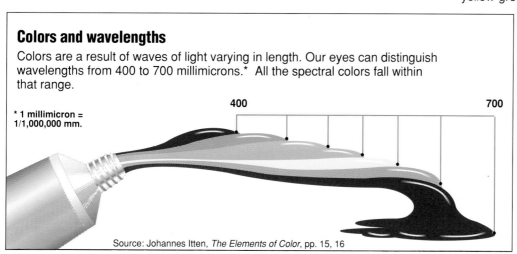

Source: Johannes Itten, *The Elements of Color*, pp. 15, 16

HARMONY AND AFTERIMAGES

Why do we call red and green "complementary" colors? What is it about that relationship (and that of yellow and purple and of blue and orange) that makes it special? Artists and interior decorators have been sensitive to these combinations for centuries. Why?

Clues to the answer can be found in the phenomenon of "afterimages." Stare at the red paint blob at the left for two minutes. Try not to blink. Then close your eyes tightly. With your eyes still closed, you should see the image of the paint blob, but it will look green, the complementary color of red. The brain cells recording the color of one image will, in its absence, project the complementary color in its place. This happens with all colors: We tend to see their complements.

In the early 1980s, there was an abundant use of two colors for text screens in newspapers: salmon and pastel blue. Look at the color wheel for a clue to why these colors were used in tandem so often.

SIMULTANEOUS CONTRAST

If we place a gray square on a larger square of color, the gray appears to take on the complement of the background color. Gray on yellow looks purplish; on orange, gray looks bluish. This phenomenon is called "simultaneous contrast" and can cause colors to shift each other toward their complements.

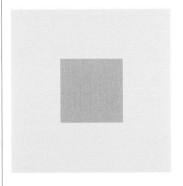

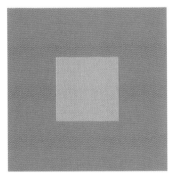

Source: Johannes Itten, *The Elements of Color*, pp. 19, 52, 53

"He who wants to become a master of color must see, feel, and experience each individual color in its endless combinations with all other colors. Colors must have a mystical capacity for spiritual expression, without being tied to objects. "

Johannes Itten
The Elements of Color

COLORS AND THEIR NEIGHBORS

We rarely see one color by itself. More often, we see colors next to or surrounded by others. Perhaps your favorite color is a certain shade of blue, and when it is surrounded by black the combination is most pleasing to your eye. But when you place that same shade of blue on a green or brown background, the shade changes according to the background. The blue has not changed, but your perception of it has. This shift in perception is important to anyone working with color on a newspaper page.

Sources for this chapter:

Josef Albers, *Interaction of Color* (New Haven: Yale Univ. Press, 1963)

R.L. Gregory, *Eye and Brain: The Psychology of Seeing*, 2nd ed. (New York: McGraw-Hill, 1973)

R.L. Gregory, *The Intelligent Eye* (New York: McGraw-Hill, 1970)

Johannes Itten, *The Elements of Color* (New York: Van Nostrand Reinhold, 1970)

Sir Isaac Newton, *Opticks* (New York: Dover, 1952)

 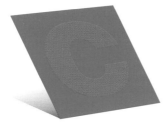 

Source: Johannes Itten, *The Elements of Color*, pp. 86, 87

How we see color

The retina is the weblike coating on the inner wall at the back of the eye. It contains photoreceptors called rods and cones (named for their shapes) that are light sensitive and convert patterns of light entering the eye into neural activity in the brain.

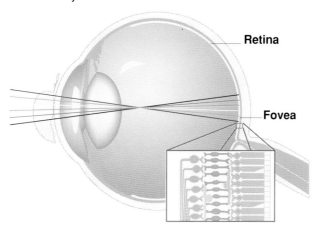

Retina

Fovea

Cones are concentrated on the fovea, where our focus and ability to see detail is greatest. Cones allow us to operate in bright daylight and to see color.

Rods are distributed across the retina. They help us see in dim light and distinguish shades of gray, but have no role in seeing color.

Sources: R.L. Gregory, *Eye and Brain*, pp. 44-48; *The Family Medical Encyclopedia*, 1987.

PHOTOS AND SCREENS

If a background or border screen for a photograph matches more than 50% of the photo's dominant color, the background will seem to merge with the photo and flatten the image. If, however, the background is in a contrasting color that recedes from the plane of the page, the photo will appear to come forward and take on a three-dimensional appearance.

POINTS OF ENTRY

How do readers travel through pages?

■ *Photos and artwork are the primary points of entry, whether they are in color or black and white.*

■ *Front-page promotion boxes generate attention from most readers.*

■ *Readers do not automatically look at the traditional top-right position for the lead story on the front page.*

■ *Readers usually enter the page through the dominant photo and then move to a prominent headline or another dominant photo.*

■ *Readers usually enter facing pages through the dominant photo on the right-hand page and then look at the dominant headline or photo on the left-hand page.*

How do readers actually "travel" around a newspaper page? According to our traditions, the first stop is the "lead story" high on the right side of the page. Textbooks have sanctified this axiom; generations of layout editors and designers have adhered to it.

But our research exposes this as a myth. When the reader enters a page, attention is drawn to *no* predetermined position.

Instead, unless readers are searching for a specific element, such as the "Peanuts" cartoon or the lead editorial in their traditional places, the reader's attention focuses first on the dominant visual element, usually a photograph or graphic, sometimes a strong headline. From that point of entry, the reader begins to deal with the rest of the information on the page.

There is no evidence that the right-hand side of the page is better than the left for the lead story position.

What's more, readers don't enter the front page with a preconceived visual map. The dominant elements of design determine the reader's route, and these elements can be affected by story content, placement, size, and color.

FRONT-PAGE ENTRY

Prototype A has three color elements on the front page. Prototype B has no color on the front page below the nameplate.

POINTS OF ENTRY: Color lead photo

Here's how readers enter the front page where the lead photo is in color. Notice that the traditional lead position, top right-hand corner, generates little traffic.

Prototype **A**, Page 1

Promos and nameplate generate 36% of the initial attention.

Only 4% enter here, the traditional lead position.

49% enter the page through the color photo.

4% enter below the fold.

Prototype A

The dominant color photo captures nearly half (49%) of all entries to the page. Only 4% enter below the fold. The lead headline in the conventional top-right position generates little attention as a point of entry. The bottom of the page is seldom used as a point of entry. After readers enter the page at the dominant photo, they tend to stay at the top of the page and look at the lead headline next.

Prototype B

Here, too, the dominant photo, although black and white, captures the most initial attention, but by a smaller margin (35%) than its color counterpart in Prototype A (49%). With less competition from a color photo, the lead headline, directly to the right, commands 18% of the point-of-entry traffic, compared with only 4% for the lead headline in Prototype A with the color photo. Even the top of the page attracts well: 24% look at the promos first; 16% look at the nameplate first.

Black and white vs. color in lead photos

When the lead color photo is the point of entry, half of the "secondary movement" (where the eye travels next after the point of entry) goes to the lead headline. When the black-and-white photo is the point of entry, secondary movement is divided almost equally between the lead headline to the right (38%) and the off-lead headline to the left (44%).

POINTS OF ENTRY: Black-and-white lead photo

Even though the lead photo is in black and white, it generates high traffic as a point of entry. The traditional lead position once again attracts little attention.

Prototype **B**, Page 1

Promos and nameplate together generate 40% of all entries.

18% enter through the lead headline.

35% enter through the lead photo.

0% enter the page below the fold.

PROMOS

Do promo boxes above the nameplate attract readers? Yes, at least in this study. What's more, the more colorful they are, the more powerful they are.

Over the last decade, as the use of promo boxes and teasers has proliferated, editors and artists have debated their efficacy. Adherents say they attract readers to the rich variety of the news pages within. Skeptics charge that routine formats with predictable landscapes desensitize readers.

Our research will not end the debate, but it may add new information on which to make judgments. For example, there is strong evidence that promos at the top of Page One generate high levels of reader traffic.

But here, too, design counts. Color helps attract, but color by itself is not enough. How the typography is presented seems to be important as well.

Because we wanted participants in the study to feel comfortable with the prototypes, each was designed to look like the local newspaper. To accomplish this, we let the local art directors use their indigenous style for the promos.

The results show a high percentage of processing (that is, most readers at least look at the promos) in all three cities. But actual "reading" (defined as eye movement across one or more lines of print from left to right) is significantly lower in the St. Petersburg test, where the promos are less colorful and more conservatively designed.

Star Tribune

The Minneapolis *Star Tribune* uses a gray box in Prototype B and a mint green box in Prototype A. Both prototypes use a peach-colored teaser box that customarily appears in the upper right-hand corner.

Taken together, a large number of readers process the promos (80%) and two-thirds actually read them (67%). These numbers confirm that there is significant reader traffic above the fold.

The Register

The Orange County Register uses a gray-blue box with a black-and-white drawing in Prototype B and a peach-colored screen with a color drawing in Prototype A.

Here, too, the teasers generate high traffic (60% average for both prototypes). More significantly, of those who first look at the promos, more than three-quarters (78%) actually read them.

Keep in mind that when testing prototypes, no matter how closely they match the local newspaper, you are almost certain to generate higher numbers than you would testing a standard newspaper. Nevertheless, the results in Minneapolis and Orange County are convincing evidence that readers can be attracted to well-designed, colorful promotions above the nameplate.

St. Petersburg Times

The *St. Petersburg Times* uses a slightly different style for its promotions: a simple two-line unit in black and white, with color used only for a yellow box that identifies the specific edition.

When this style is tested, a curious thing happens. Although processing is high (67% looked at the teasers), reading is far lower than in the other cities (25%).

PROMO BOXES

Promo boxes in each paper attract a lot of attention. The more colorful and graphic promos are read more than the type-only promos.

"Colors present themselves in continuous flux, constantly related to changing neighbors and changing conditions."

Josef Albers
The Interaction of Color

29

It is part of the conventional wisdom of our craft that readers look at only one page at a time. Our research may put this notion on a growing pile of myths about newspaper design.

Origins of the myth are not hard to fathom. Broadsheet newspaper pages are rather large, so it makes intuitive sense that a reader deals with facing pages as completely separate units.

Accepting that notion, we seldom design facing pages as a single unit, except, of course, if we're working on a special two-page spread or double-truck in the centerspread position. In fact, a page's designer may be unaware of the content of the facing page. Inevitably, clashes and conflicts occur. But the practice of thinking in single pages continues.

Most of the literature of newspaper design slights the subject and simply accepts as axiomatic the one-page-at-a-time approach.

Our study reveals that a reader's entry into the inside of a newspaper occurs as a quick sweep across the canvas of two pages. Furthermore, that trajectory not only crosses the page boundaries, but it can be altered by the positioning of dominant visual elements. The implications for page designers are important.

Playing an important role in the reader's movement across facing pages is the hierarchy of the elements on the pages. The dominant element, often a large

Entry into facing inside pages occurs across the canvas of both pages.

photograph, is usually the first stop in this journey. The next largest or most dominant editorial element is usually the second stop.

The research uncovers another surprise. Intuition tells us that in the English language moving left to right across a page or series of pages is the most "natural." The study, however, shows that entry on the right page with movement to the left is more common.

Color contributes to dominance; so does size. So when an element is large and in color, it's a sure bet to attract initial or secondary attention and to play a role in guiding eye movement across the two pages.

EFFECT OF BLACK-AND-WHITE PHOTOS

When black-and-white photos are on facing pages, the point of entry is usually determined by size. In this study the point of entry is most often the dominant photo on the right-hand page, whether in color or black and white. From there the trajectory usually is across the spread to the dominant photo on the left-hand page.

There are exceptions to this norm, however. In two cases we find readers moving left to right. In one, all the photos are black and white. In the other, the right-hand photo is in color and the left is black and white. In both cases, the dominant photos are either very active sports images or large, expressive faces.

The following pages illustrate the findings.

The movement is a sort of quick trajectory that depends on the positioning and strength of visual elements.

If you looked here first, then moved to the large #2 on the left-hand page, your behavior followed that of the majority of readers in the study. The most common eye movement across two facing pages is from right to left. Color and size are the dominant factors affecting this movement.

Prototype **A**, Pages 2 & 3

One dominant image

A dominant image in color on a right-hand page is a strong contender for the reader's initial attention, especially if the dominant photo on the left-hand page is in black and white. If both are in color (bottom), size and content come into play, along with position.

Prototype **B**, Pages 2 & 3

Prototype **A**, Pages 12 & 13

Two dominant images

In this example the two color photos compete almost equally for attention.

Prototype **B**, Pages 18 & 19

Two photos prevail. . .

When two photos appear on the left-hand page, they attract more point-of-entry attention than the single color photo on the right-hand page.

Prototype **A**, Pages 18 & 19

. . . even when black and white

This happens even when the left-hand pair is black and white. The active content of the sports photos on the left may be a factor.

Prototype **A**, Pages 10 & 11

Prototype **B**, Pages 10 & 11

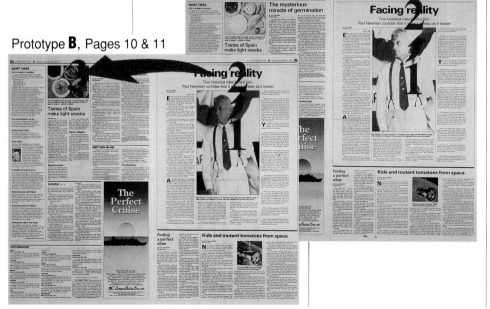

But don't count out color

In Prototype A, the dominant black-and-white photo on the right attracts initial attention. From there, most readers move to the strong headline above.

But look what happens when a small photograph on the left-hand page is in color (Prototype B). The point of entry is still the dominant photograph on the right, but now the secondary movement goes to the headline and then over to the color photo.

Prototype A, Pages 6 & 7

Watch for exceptions

When the snake photo is in color (Prototype A), it dominates. Secondary movement is across to the photo on the far left.

Prototype B, Pages 6 & 7

But when the snake photo is in black and white (Prototype B), readers head for the far-left photo first and then move to the cutline, avoiding the snake altogether. Part of the reason for this may be the poor quality of the snake photo in black and white.

Prototype B, Pages 4 & 5

Prototype A, Pages 4 & 5

Right to left

The predominant movement on facing pages is right to left, particularly if a strong color image is the point of entry on the far right. (Prototype B)

This right-to-left movement can buck strong competition, as in Prototype A where readers enter the pages at the black-and-white photo despite the presence of two color photos on the left-hand page.

Ads vs. news

As far as attracting attention, there is no contest in this study between ads and news. Ads are never the point of entry on a page, even when in color.

Color alone is not enough

On facing pages with color in advertising but not in editorial material, the black-and-white photos are the points of entry, not the color ads. The closest an ad comes to gaining much attention is the Delta Airlines ad in color (Prototype A), and even then, it gets the second look, not the first.

Prototype **A**, Pages 8 & 9

Does a full page help?

Not in this study. The "lobster" overpowers the ad as a point of entry, although when the ad is in color, it does becomes a secondary stop. But when the ad is in black and white, secondary movement is to the headline below the lobster.

Prototype **B**, Pages 8 & 9

HIERARCHY

What we have explored in this section should re-mind us of a simple principle of design: Create a hierarchy. The object of good publication design is to first attract the readers, and then guide them through the information. Too many newspapers abandon readers by turning them loose to wan-der through the fields and forests of the unfamil-iar. No wonder so many readers are perplexed and eventually lost. By creating a hierarchy of movement through a page or across facing pages, we can coach and counsel readers gently but ef-fectively, establishing a harmony of movement that results in comprehension. To plan this jour-ney for others, we first need to see as the reader sees—in this case, two pages at a time.

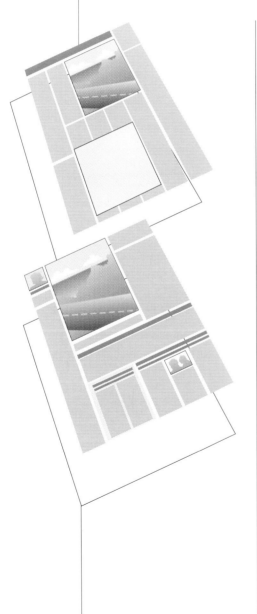

No sense of hierarchy here

Similar shapes in similar places on similar pages soon gets boring, like this sentence. In this example, the designer serves up am-biguity and indecision. Noth-ing is facilitated except con-fusion.

Contrast establishes hierarchy

Contrast creates the tension that propels a reader from one element to the next. Just as color is a tool of con-trast, so are size and shape.

SEQUENCE

So far, we have established that there are some "natural" sequences of eye movement, from the right side to the left, from a strong color to black and white, from the largest element to something smaller. But once accepted, this wisdom is meant to be used creatively, not followed slavishly into formula-driven formats. Strong elements of color, size, and shape can be manipulated at will in deliberate attempts to alter traditional patterns. Or, they can reinforce conventions that have worked well for years. Either way, we must understand that sequence is important and recognize the valuable tools at hand to establish that sequence.

READING

What do readers process?

■ *Headlines, cutlines, and briefs are processed often and in depth in this study.*

■ *Only 25% of the text is processed.*

■ *Text processing is highest in the news section, lowest in sports.*

■ *Color screens have no impact on how much text is read.*

■ *Readers seem to prefer colorful pages over more muted pages.*

To better understand this chapter, it's best to run the gauntlet of a glossary one more time. Familiar terms like "processing" and "reading" have special meaning here.

■ **Processing opportunity.** Every element in the prototypes represents an opportunity for that element to be looked at, or "processed." Therefore, every headline, photo, cutline, and story is a "processing opportunity."

■ **Processing.** An element is "processed" when a reader looks at it. That's all; just looks. To "process" something, the reader's attention stops long enough at an individual element—a cutline, photo, or bit of text—for information to be acquired, or "processed."

■ **Reading**. If the reader's eyes move across one or more lines of print from left to right, the material is considered "read."

■ **In-depth reading.** When at least half of any text is read, it is considered read "in depth."

HEADLINES

Headlines are designed to get attention. And in this study, they do.

■ More than half the headlines in the prototypes are processed—twice the processing level of text.

■ The presence of photographs makes a difference. Headline reading is greater when either black-and-white or color photos are nearby.

Headlines, photos, and illustrations are the main points of entry on most pages. The larger the headline, the more attention it gets. When photos are nearby, headline attention increases.

BRIEFS

Two-thirds of the briefs boxes are processed and about half of the individual items are read. Color on briefs boxes has no impact on processing.

- Size, too, makes a difference. As you might expect, one-column heads are less likely to be seen than multi-column heads.

- Males and females process headlines similarly, except in sports, where male processing is higher.

- Headlines and photos share equally as the targets of secondary eye movements.

BRIEFS

Briefs are popular with readers. Two-thirds of all briefs boxes (an aggregation of individual brief items) are processed, and most of the briefs within the boxes are read.

When color screens are placed over the boxes, there is no difference in reader processing. (We discuss color screens in more detail later in this chapter.)

TEXT

As expected, text is not processed or read as much as photographs or headlines, the page's attention-getters and natural points of entry. In this study, the typical participant processes anywhere from half to nearly all the photos and heads. Because headlines and photographs filter readers' interests into or away from text, processing of text is expected to be lower. In this study it is: About 25% of all text is processed.

Of that processed text, however, 50% is read in depth. The statistics for processing and reading in depth are similar across news, features, and sports sections.

Although photographs attract attention, they are no guarantee that readers will process accompanying text. For example, the sports photos on the left-hand page of the facing pages below are the point of entry for both pages. But the text that accompanies those photos is hardly processed at all.

Males in this study process more sports stories, females slightly more features. Males read slightly more in depth, but not enough to begin, much less settle, any arguments on the subject.

PHOTOS AND TEXT

Here's an example where readers enter facing pages through two sports photos. Even though the photos are strong magnets (in black and white or color), the accompanying text draws very little attention.

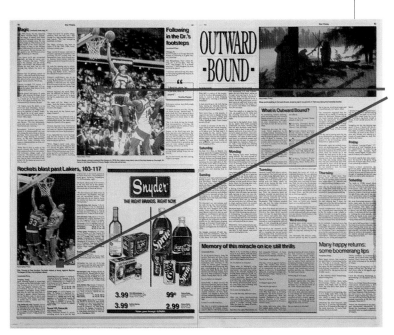

After entering these facing pages through the photos, readers process very little of the accompanying text.

COLOR AND READING

Color seems to have little impact on text in these results. For example, having a color (as opposed to a black-and-white) photo accompanying a story does not increase reading of the text.

TEXT AND COLOR SCREENS

A recent addition to conventional wisdom about design has cast doubts on the use of color screens over text. Many argue that screens reduce legibility and therefore comprehension. Some newspapers have banned their use. Others have restricted screens to light mixes of color, often sand and light blue.

This study tested light blue, gray, magenta, peach, yellow, and purple. We included the purple, magenta, and yellow to juxtapose garish colors against more subtle tones. Our expectation was that readers would prefer the subtle to the garish.

To our surprise, it doesn't seem to make any difference. Screened text is processed the same as unscreened text. And in most cases, that is true no matter which color is tested. Nor do screens affect points of entry. On pages displaying large color screens over text, photos and headlines remain the dominant points of entry regardless of the screens.

One variation on this theme deserves mention. When a magenta screen is compared with a yellow screen, both are processed (looked at) to similar degrees, but the in-depth reading of the magenta-screened text is significantly higher.

Still, the general conclusions remain: Screens don't seem to affect text processing in any predictable ways.

IS LESS COLOR BEST?

If color is a good thing, is more of a good thing even better? How much is too much? How do readers respond to extensive, even excessive, use of color?

To test this issue, we over-colored the "lobster story" in Prototype A, deploying a purple screen and red headline opposite a full-page color ad. (You can see the pages on the insert.) It's a powerful package indeed. For comparison, Prototype B is colorful but tamer. Its lobster illustration stands alone with subtle sand colors. The ad is in black and white.

WHAT READERS REPORT

When asked what pages they like, readers choose the more colorful pages over the more muted pages. The color screens over the text have little impact on processing and reading.

After participants were tested with the EYE-TRAC® Research equipment, we put the two pages side by side and asked them to comment as part of their exit interview. The majority liked the more colorful page, explaining that the color attracted attention. Results of the EYE-TRAC® Research itself tell a less dramatic story. The more colorful page does draw slightly more attention, but reading of the pages is comparable.

A similar thing happened on Page 20. In each city a local story was displayed with a color photo surrounded by a blue screen. One prototype has a black-and-white ad beneath, the other a color ad. Again, af-

ter the formal testing readers were asked to compare the two. The more colorful page was the favorite in all three cities, with many participants reporting that color made the text easier to read.

The same page tested with EYE-TRAC® Research was less conclusive. Readers seemed to process the less colorful pages slightly more. That may not be a result of color, because this was the one page in the prototypes that varied in content from city to city.

PROMOS

Each newspaper developed its own style and content for the promotional material. Testing these differences, we find readers are more attracted to the Minneapolis *Star Tribune* promotions than to those in the *St. Petersburg Times* or *The Orange County Register.* As for actual reading of the

teasers, it is very high in Orange County (78%) and Minnesota (67%), but low in St. Petersburg (25%).

On the "lobster" page, St. Petersburg and Orange County placed teasers at the bottom of the page. Minneapolis placed teasers at the top, where they attracted far more attention than the promos at the bottom.

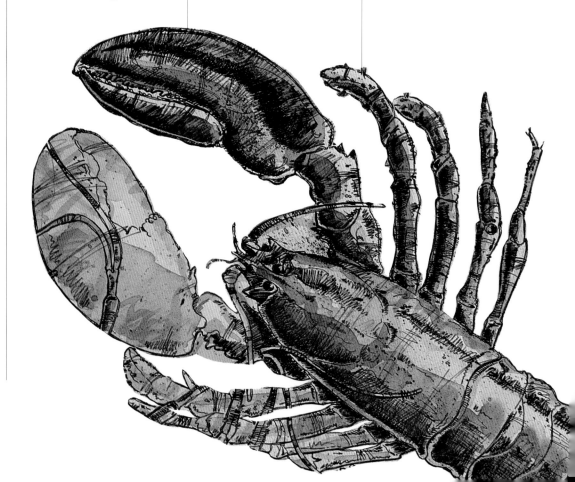

Research challenges editors' myths about how readers actually read

Photos and headlines attract, so does color. But most text is by-passed. Can design help?

■ **Johnny can read; he just doesn't very much**, despite the powerful attraction of graphic elements. If people are "scanners" instead of readers, have we made it easy for them? Does our newsroom structure get in the way?

■ **Design can make a difference.** And "design" must include how we organize our writing. The inverted pyramid should be abandoned; we need to develop new devices to inform readers.

■ **New writing styles are needed.** We need to get beyond the dispatch and the essay to new forms of presenting information.

Johnny can read; he just doesn't

Why don't readers read? We know they look at most of the photographs, nearly all the artwork, a high percentage of the headlines. But the falloff from the graphics to the text is dramatic.

The gap is actually worse than this study suggests. Testing prototypes invariably produces higher, more positive numbers than testing "real" newspapers. The reasons are simple. The prototypes are smaller, thus easier to read. The copy is cleaner (it's been edited for weeks), and the layouts are less cluttered.

Still, you'd think people would read more text.

Not necessarily. Our colleague at The Poynter Institute, Don Fry, is not disturbed at all by the finding.

"I don't divide the world into 'loyal readers' and 'scanners,'" Don tells us. "I suspect all readers are scanners."

If that's so, it's clear that most newspapers are not designed to meet the needs of scanners. To be sure, some newspapers deploy various devices for the scanner: indexes, digest of world briefs, and the like. They nod their heads automatically when designers talk about "multiple points of entry to a page." But the truth is, editors and their comrades in the art department have not been successful in using design elements to increase readership of text.

Part of the problem may be the way we organize the work. We segregate and isolate crafts. Reporters write stories, but seldom have anything to do with the accompanying photograph or headline, two critical elements that we know are powerful attractors of reader attention. The headline is usually written by someone seeing the story for the first time.

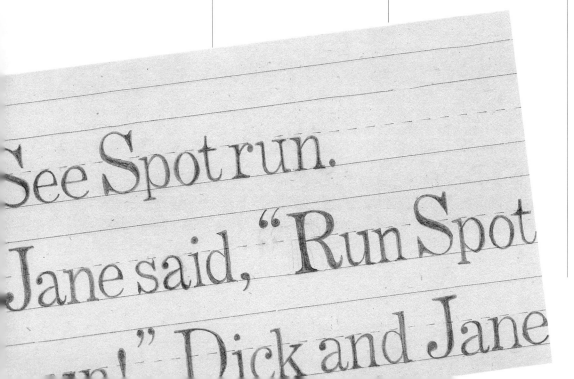

Photographers are often assigned to take pictures without seeing the story, or even discussing it with the writer. Photo editors further removed from the original creative tasks "edit" the photos; layout editors or designers even more remote from the source govern display decisions. No wonder the result is often a jumble of confused patterns that repel rather than attract readers.

Design can make a difference

Powerful graphic elements get attention. Can those elements be used to increase readership?

Here's how design can help:

1 We need to get away from the tyranny of the inverted pyramid, an ancient and venerated device that Don Fry thinks is boring if not downright destructive. "If scanners enter a story wherever they happen to land, then text immediately following these points of entry must have 'lead' quality." Good point, but that's not how most stories are written. The inverted pyramid still has power, turning upside-down our ability to accommodate the scanners.

2 Another hot-metal hangover is the lead story in the upper-right position. This study demonstrates readers will go first to the dominant element on the

page (usually a photograph), making the lead story concept a relic of another age. The lead story is wherever we design it to be.

3 The only benefit of the inverted pyramid lead was that it put a lot of valuable information high in the story. Some papers are learning to do that with more effective heads and deck heads. The *St. Petersburg*

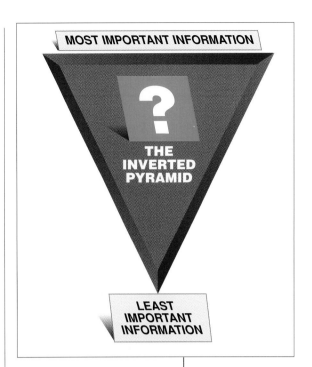

A SUGGESTION

A simple example of a new way to present information is the format of these pages. Instead of the conventional headline over body type, we've used:
✔ A main head
✔ A deck to expand the head
✔ Color-coded summaries of the three parts, or modules, of the story
✔ Subheads and summaries at each module
✔ A numbering system where appropriate
✔ A closing box of more information

Times calls these devices "blurbettes." Others call them "nut graphs." Whatever the name, the device works, as numerous European newspapers have demonstrated for years.

We think variations like this—and the dozens of others creative editors and designers could invent— can help attract and hold readers.

MOST IMPORTANT INFORMATION

?

THE INVERTED PYRAMID

LEAST IMPORTANT INFORMATION

Evaku
dansk

Danskere i Ira

Udenrigsministeriet arbejder i øjeblikket på at få de strandede danskere i...
me...

Once again, NASA see
source of shuttle leak

■ Next month, the agency will try another launch — with a different shuttle. Officials say *Discovery* is ...uffer the

gen is at its coldest — below zero Fahrenhe...

Officials think linked to the disman bia after its last fl Workers took a compartment in a tamination by a n...

New writing styles are needed

Readers are attracted by graphics, but too few proceed into the accompanying text. Design can help, but first we must abandon cherished practices.

Despite the rich variety of styles and formats in the English language, newspapers have limited themselves to a couple of old favorites: the "telegraphic dispatch" in news, and the essay in editorials and analysis. We try to sing a complex chorus of information with a few baritones and no tenors or sopranos.

As we learn to arrange the information more effectively, we will be forced to vary our writing styles and aim more for the needs of the readers than for the whims of the contest judges. For example, consider the conventional thinking about transitions. "Most teachers and textbooks present them as invisible bridges from one sentence, paragraph, or section to the next," Don Fry reminds us. "If all readers scan, transitions need to have lead quality, and they need to be visible rather than 'smooth as glass.'"

Cutline style might have to be reconsidered. We know photographs are the dominant attractors to a page. Doesn't it make sense, then, to consider expanding the cutline format wherever appropriate, on occasion even putting the entire "story" into the caption?

Pope John Paul II concluded his 10-day trip to the United States with a visit to Detroit September 18-19. He held mass in the Cathedral of the Most Blessed Sacrament on Friday night and gave a speech to thousands in downtown Detroit on Saturday. The pope's message emphasized social progress and human development. He told the crowds, "The best traditions of your land presume respect for those who cannot defend themselves." Pope John will travel to Canada before returning to Rome.

Finally, we must use the no-longer-new computer technology to write, edit, and revise text and designs in new ways. Few newspapers have taken full advantage of these tools. We still tend to do old tasks with new tools instead of devising new applications for the new tools.

WHAT YOU CAN DO

 ■ Understand readers' eye patterns.

 ■ Design for the "scanner."

 ■ Review this new research on color.

 ■ Experiment!

Having gathered participants for some high-tech probing using EYE-TRAC® Research equipment, we couldn't resist the temptation to do some old-fashioned interviewing.

We were curious about reader preferences for colors and screens, and about their opinions of story content and length.

After the EYE-TRAC® Research tests, in which an individual reader saw only one of the prototypes, we showed participants *both* prototypes and asked them to make some comparisons.

This is not research you can project beyond the limits of this particular study, but it does provide some useful insights. We report no numbers from these exit interviews, only our general observations.

■ Readers seem to prefer more color.

■ They are much less aware of tinted screens than we might expect. Furthermore, in some cases they say they prefer the brighter or more garish colors. In any case, the screens affect neither processing nor reading.

■ The stories that readers tell us they like the most are usually, in fact, the ones they read most in the actual test.

■ When they tell us they think a story is too long, their low processing of the story confirms that opinion.

Combining the thoughts and preferences of readers with the results of the test, we find additional evidence for a gap between what readers think and do and what editors *believe* readers think and do.

For example, most editors believe readers automatically enter facing pages on the left-hand page and move right. They don't. Most editors think headlines are as compelling as photographs. They aren't.

Our suggestion to editors, then, is to reconsider some of the myths and traditions of the craft, and to use the findings of this and other studies to reassess cherished axioms about how readers actually use a newspaper so we can construct better-working designs.

EXIT INTERVIEWS

WHAT READERS LIKE

When asked after the testing what stories and color selections they like, the majority of readers rank "Dear Abby," "Ann Landers," and the more colorful pages very high.

PHOTOS & ART

How do readers respond to photos?

■ *Color does not necessarily draw more attention to photos.*

■ *Photos and artwork generate more processing by readers than do headlines or text. In addition, they are the main points of entry on most pages.*

■ *Readers devote more time to photo groupings when they are in color.*

■ *Size increases the attraction to a photo.*

■ *Fewer than half of the mug shots are processed by readers in this study.*

The photographs in the prototypes fall into two categories: 1) those that *don't* change from black and white to color between prototypes as we test other elements, and 2) those that *do* change as we test the impact of color on the photographs themselves.

Consequently, our analysis of photographs is in two parts. The first reviews the overall processing of *all* photographs, whether they changed or not. The second part analyzes those photographs that were black and white in one prototype and color in the other.

OVERALL PROCESSING

Photos attract attention. They are the dominant point of entry on nearly every page, only occasionally sharing that role with headlines. Overall, 75% of the photos are processed.

This high level of processing holds true whether the photo is in black and white or color.

Size

If it's true that photos attract attention, it's also true that big photos attract more attention. We find, to no one's surprise, a link between size and reader processing of photographs. Fewer than half the mug shots are processed (45%), but nearly all the photos of three columns or more are processed (92%).

Furthermore, we detect a large increase in processing between one- and two-column pictures.

In most cases, photos (black and white or color) are the main points of entry.

Categories

Do news photographs command more attention than feature photos? Are images of familiar newsmakers more compelling to readers than anonymous faces?

To test these questions, we designed the prototypes with seven categories of photographs:

1. **News**

2. **Features**

3. **Mug shots**

4. **Recognizable newsmakers** are people who have been in the news before and are instantly recognized by most readers. George Bush is a good example.

5. **Unfamiliar newsmakers** are people who are in the news today, but are not recognized because they haven't been prominent before. The female soldier on the front page is an example.

6. **People with expressions** are those whose facial expressions can be seen clearly. The photo of Alex Rocco is an example.

7. **People without expression**s are those whose faces are not visible. The Outward Bound photo is an example.

Some photos fit more than one category. The Alex Rocco photo is categorized under both "features" and "people with expressions."

Before the actual tests, we speculated that certain categories would score higher in reader attention. We believed news would outpull features, that people with expressions would be in-

herently more interesting than those without, and that recognizable newsmakers would attract more attention than unfamiliar folk.

The results are interesting. Readers process all the photos in similar ways. What's more, the presence of color does not seem to make a difference within categories, that is, "unfamiliar newsmakers" are just as unfamiliar in color as they are in black and white.

CATEGORY EXAMPLES

Outward Bound photo categorized as "people without expressions."

Alex Rocco photo categorized as both "features" and "people with expressions."

The only exceptions to this "flat curve" are mug shots. They generate considerably less attention than all other categories. This could be a function of size. Or, perhaps mug shots are just boring.

We should add a word of caution about these findings. First of all, the sample is very small in each category. That doesn't mean these results are wrong; it means we have to be careful about how we use them.

Furthermore, this is a new area of research. We know of no other studies that attempt to ascertain readership of these categories, so we have no data to test against. We offer the findings not as precise conclusions, but as markers on the path for future research.

Sections

Overall, color photos in news and sports are processed more than black-and-white photos. But feature photographs show no such difference. The likelihood of a feature photo being processed by readers is the same for color and black and white.

"Great news photos distill the confused brew of human affairs."

Photojournalism
(Time-Life Books)

Gender

Do men and women react to color photos differently? Sometimes, but then only slightly. Females seem to be more likely to look at a color photo. An exception to this not-so-hard-and-fast rule is in the sports section, where color increases processing for both males and females. In features the color doesn't appear to have much impact on either males or females.

Test site

The location of the tests doesn't seem to affect the results. Readers react to photographs similarly in all three sites. The only slight differences are in California, where participants in the test process fewer photographs overall, and in Minnesota, where they process more color than black and white.

Cutlines and color

Cutlines accompanying color photographs are more likely to be processed than those accompanying black-and-white photos. (We do not find this to be true in tests with photos that change from black and white to color between prototypes.) This result is more pronounced in news and sports sections, and not evident at all in features.

The larger the photo (up to three columns), the more likely it is to be processed by readers. This also applies to the accompanying cutline. Color in the photograph doesn't influence cutline processing until the photo is three columns wide or larger; then processing is enhanced.

CUTLINE PROCESSING

Photos and cutlines are popular. As the photo size increases, so does the cutline processing. And if the photo is in color, it can attract even more attention to the cutline.

PHOTOS THAT CHANGE

The study contains numerous photographs printed in black and white in one prototype and in color in the other. These comparisons enable us to sharpen our focus on the impact of color in newspaper photography.

We find little difference in the overall results. Three-quarters of all the photos that change between prototypes are processed by the typical reader: 78% black and white, 81% color.

Size

We've already seen how size increases the chances of reader processing. This is true when the photo is in color, but no more true than when the photo is in black and white.

A one-column photo is processed to a similar degree whether it is in color or black and white. This applies up the scale.

Gender

As might be expected, males process sports photos more than females do, and that difference exists only for the black-and-white photos. The color sports photos are processed equally by males and females.

In news and feature sections, we find no differences in how males and females process photos printed in black and white in one prototype and color in the other.

Test sites

There are no geographic differences in this part of the study. Readers in Minneapolis, Orange County, and St. Petersburg show the same patterns of readership when black-and-white photos are tested against color counterparts.

Groups of photos

Page 13 of each prototype tests a package of photos of Bermuda. One prototype uses the photos in color, the other in black and white. Color is a clear winner here. Not only does color increase the chance of the package being processed, it also increases the in-depth reading of the text.

PHOTO GROUPS

The increased processing of cutlines with color photos in groups is significant. Reading of text also increases when the photos in the group are in color.

"But there's a kind of power thing about the camera. I mean everyone knows you've got some edge. You're carrying some slight magic which does something to them. It fixes them in a way."

Diane Arbus

Cutlines

We find no difference in cutline processing as a result of the switch from black-and-white to color photos.

INFORMATIONAL GRAPHIC

We tested only one informational graphic, "High-Tech Weapons." It was printed only in black and white, although the accompanying photograph was tested in color as well as in black and white.

The graphic generates the same high response (73%) whether its companion photo is in color or not.

ARTWORK

Artwork attracts. The three pieces in the prototypes—the lobster, Chris Evert, and Magic Johnson—have a high level of processing (87%). Color does not affect the high level of processing, but the size of the artwork may be exerting such a strong influence that the color doesn't make a difference.

APPLICATIONS

It is no surprise to learn that readers process photographs more than other elements in these prototypes. The power of newspaper photography has been well documented for decades, and page designers and layout editors have responded accordingly by using large photos and groups of photos to draw readers into packages of information.

This study, however, offers some clues as to how we might use these powerful tools.

Photos are the dominant element attracting readers into the page. Once drawn in by a photo, the reader is likely to move next to another photo. What's most interesting is that this is usually true whether the photo is in color or black and white. As newspapers have accumulated the technology and know-how to publish color, many editors have concluded that a color photo is always preferable to a black-and-white. This isn't so. This study demonstrates not only the drawing power of photographs, but also the often overlooked power of black-and-white photographs.

Another lesson is the importance of content. The group of Bermuda photos attracts more attention in color than in black and white. Why? We suspect that content has a lot to do with it. Bermuda has a colorfulness apparent even to those who have never been there. So color is an appropriate medium to use when depicting Bermuda, and readers respond accordingly.

In another case, however, we find that the front-page photo of the female Army officer draws the same reader reaction in black and white as it does in color. Is it because color is not important to the content of that story? Or does a large front-page photograph have such power that it can draw attention in color or black and white?

Decisions about color versus black and white may have to begin with other factors, particularly content. If color seems more appropriate to the subject, or if it somehow enhances or explains the story with greater clarity or precision, then it is a good choice.

Often these decisions are political. How many times is color used simply because it's available on that page, or because the company has just spent millions on new color presses? In the real world these reasons are understandable, but they may not contribute much to readers' understanding of the day's news.

A better justification is found in the competitive publishing environment we all work in. Readers are accustomed to color in everything from magazine advertising to MTV. To use no color at all, or worse, to use color badly, is to diminish a newspaper's image with its audience.

> "The use of color implies a knowledge, or at least an awareness, not only of the mechanics of color, but also of the formal, psychological, and cultural problems involved. Color cannot be separated from its physical environment without changing."
>
> **Paul Rand**
> *A Designer's Art*

COLOR IN THE 90s

COLOR IN THE 90s

Newspapers have always been inspired by their surroundings. Gray was an appropriate look in the days of radio and black-and-white movies. When films, and later television, put color in their cheeks, newspapers followed suit, at least in the Sunday comics.

And what wonderful colors they were—bright, brassy, boisterous primary colors that shouted and strutted and laughed across otherwise still-gray pages.

By the 1980s we had abandoned the primaries for more subtle shades. Newspapers began to look like our living rooms, filled with pastels, earth tones, mint greens, and soft lavenders. This softening of our color palette became a habit as we retreated into a narrow range of tones.

The reigning monarch of the era was Pacific Salmon—10% yellow, 10% magenta. Salmon was to newspaper color of the 1980s what Bodoni was to typography of the 1890s.

But monarchs don't reign long in these egalitarian days, so the salmon era was bound to spawn something else. Fortunately, old regimes have a way of returning to the throne. Look at Carmen Miranda, that wonderfully energetic Brazilian musical film star. Her fruity hats in eye-popping colors have been hopelessly outdated since her brief reign in the 1940s.

But those colors are back. We may not be ready to do a three-color samba on every page, but we have rediscovered what Carmen knew all along—colorful is happier. And we may be catching up to our readers on this bit of wisdom. How else do you explain readers' preference for the "lobster" page in its most exaggerated version?

Not only is Carmen Miranda's fruity crown of colors back in favor, Dick Tracy's trenchcoat has made an even greater comeback. It's no small irony that we again turn to the comics for color inspiration as a venerable character steps out of the newspaper page and onto the movie screen to become a graphic image for an age.

And once again we discover the primaries. Colors compete with characters for top billing in the movie *Dick Tracy.* Tracy's yellow raincoat is a star worthy of its own dressing room and agent. Yellow, that wonderful stuff of sunlight and goodness, is a color fit for a hero. Faithful girlfriend Tess is painted in warm colors. The gang of baddies— Big Boy, Pruneface, and Breathless—are attired in blue, indigo, and violet. Art imitates art to create a life of its own. Newspaper designers should see the movie and take notes.

PEANUTS

Charles M. Schulz

THIS IS ALWAYS A DIFFICULT GREEN TO READ...

MAYBE I SHOULD WAIT FOR IT TO COME OUT IN PAPERBACK..

5-10

The trend doesn't begin and end with *Dick Tracy*. Spanish filmmaker Pedro Almodovar paints his screens from a vivid palette of reds and other primary colors. *Woman on the Verge of a Nervous Breakdown* and *Tie Me Up! Tie Me Down!* would have no impact at all in subtle tones. The color is another character in the plot.

And the reggae look still reverberates. One fashion magazine, seeking the perfect look, suggested that "for a pure bohemian body wrap, layer a blazing sarong over fuchsia balloon pants. Accompany it with a bold striped top and some multi-color festive chains and belts to finish off the flamboyant look..."

This is the environment newspapers are working in today. Are we suggesting you "layer a blazing sarong over fuchsia pants" on the front page? Of course not, but we *do* suggest your readers may be primed for bolder colors.

We leave you with two thoughts about dealing with this more vivid environment of color:

■ Strong colors are difficult to reproduce. It was easy to get Pacific Salmon above the threshold of quality control, which may have accounted for its popularity. It's not at all easy to do a bright red. A mushy, washed-out red, yes. But a bright red? That's difficult.

 So don't let your ego and drive to be contemporary get too far ahead of your ability to print quality color. Work on the notes and basic steps before you sing and dance on pages with bright colors.

Ric Ferro

■ Don't be so timid. Like the chef who alters his creation with a bit more spice, put more color condiments into your delicacies. Be careful and selective, but be a bit more adventurous. If we learned anything during this study, it is that readers just might tolerate, even encourage, more excitement and innovation from us. So why not give it to them?

Mario R. Garcia

W, July 2-16, 1990

SOME RESEARCH SUGGESTIONS

In the early 1980s, when I surveyed 112 front-page editors about design principles and practices[1], I observed that many design decisions are based on tradition and intuition. There's nothing wrong with that as long as the editor's intuition is the same as the reader's habits. But as we try to confirm that correlation through research, we often find a gap between how the editor thinks readers read the newspaper and how they actually read it.

For example, when asked in that survey where the lead story of the day was placed, about half said top right and the rest said top left and top center. When asked why, the majority replied that readers expect the lead story to be in that position and so look there first. Could it be that readers in one part of the country are conditioned to look right for the lead story and readers in another market are conditioned to look left or center? Perhaps. But, after we analyzed actual reading patterns in this study, we found that few readers actually enter the page through the traditional lead position, whether it's top right or top left.

Content and design decisions are usually made by editors on behalf of what they perceive readers' needs to be. What editors need is additional research to refine those perceptions. For example, for years the conventional wisdom decreed that newspapers should be written on an eighth-grade level. Today that old saw is appropriate only for our eighth-grade readers. To be sure, some readers could not comprehend that level, but most of those probably aren't readers anyway. At the other end, every newspaper has within its general readership people with fluency and expertise in various areas. They may stumble through an obtuse piece on the economy but soar through a complex article on their particular field. The point is that when we write and design, we can't assume one level of comprehension any more than we can assume a uniform level of interest.

Therefore, because readers are not all "eighth-graders," we have to write and design for the whole school, not just one grade. That means paying more attention to: 1) whether color can enhance comprehension, 2) how much knowledge people bring to the newspaper, and 3) how readers feel about their newspapers.

Color and comprehension

Can color increase comprehension? We don't know. We do know that color can help attract attention, that in some cases it might even encourage a bit more reading, but we can't equate these phenomena with comprehension.

But we could find out with more research. By looking at pages with photos that change from black and white in one version to color in the other, we could begin testing not just for "processing" or "reading," but for actual comprehension. The same techniques could test the effectiveness of devices often used in

Our study shows that readers do not enter the front page through the traditional lead story position, top right or top left, as some editors might think.

maps and informational graphics. For example, would a color version of a Middle East map showing troop movements or changing economic conditions be better read and, more important, better understood if the map used red arrows for troop movements, color screens over text, and color-coded numbers guiding the readers through the complex sequence of information?

Intuitively we believe these devices enhance understanding, but we don't know how or why. Research can help us find out.

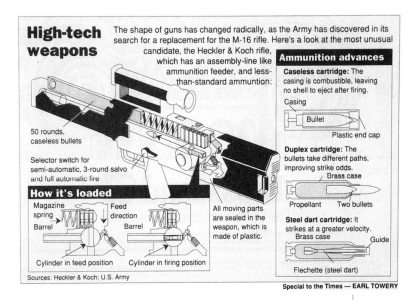

Would the addition of color as a directional device to guide the reader through the graphic help the reader better understand the information?

What readers bring to the newspaper

There has been a lot of research on what newspapers bring to readers, but very little on what kind of knowledge readers have as they use their newspaper. Clearly, some readers know more about a story than others. How do we write and design for the "experts" *and* for the "nonexperts"?

In this study we were surprised that different photo categories do not attract more processing. But I think that's a result of how we conducted this study. We were testing for the effect of color. We didn't test for participants' familiarity with a subject before reading a story or their comprehension afterward.

Would the photo of Bruce Springstein on Page 3 be a main point of entry if the rock star were less familiar? Our study suggests that it doesn't seem to matter, but I'm convinced that additional research will uncover links between what people know and like and what they eventually read and comprehend.

Readers and feelings

Finally, we need more research on emotional reactions. Does color, with its tones and intensity, create deeper feelings about a subject? Does color make a photo more "realistic," and therefore more credible? We know readers can have an emotional response to a particularly sensitive photograph. How does color affect that response?

These are just three areas of possible research that have emerged from our EYE-TRAC® Research project. Common to all these suggestions is helping editors close the gap between their own intuitions and what readers actually want and need from the newspaper.

Pegie Stark

[1.] Pegie Stark, *Newspaper Design Principles and Practices* (Indiana University dissertation, 1985).

DISCUSSION

What have we learned from all this? Have we helped newspapers that want to improve their use of color? The authors invited several colleagues on the Poynter faculty to go beyond the raw data and wrestle with the implications of the findings. They were joined in that task by Dr. Sharon Polansky, who managed the EYE-TRAC® Research. What follows is an edited conversation about the implications of the study for newspaper designers and managers.

Mario Garcia

Pegie Stark

Ed Miller

Don Fry

Sharon Polansky

ED: We know color is a powerful tool. Is it always preferable to black and white?

MARIO: Not at all. One of the notions we help de-mythologize in this study is the idea that color dominates in all circumstances. It doesn't.

PEGIE: For example, we find that a black-and-white photo can outpull a color photo. We find that size can have as much effect on eye movements as color. We learn that a right-to-left movement is the prevailing pattern across two pages, not a left-to-right, and that that movement can override a strong tendency to look at the color first. So, powerful as it is, color is not always "better" in the sense of being a more powerful magnet for readers' attention.

MARIO: We also see that color didn't seem to help the advertising in the prototypes, at least in terms of drawing readers to look at the ads first. That never happens, even when the ads employ strong color up against editorial black and white.

ED: Is that a function of advertising?

SHARON: No. In the first place, this project wasn't designed to study advertising. Where we have done studies of advertising in other places, we have found that advertising is usually not the point of entry anyway, so that's not a surprise here. Also, we have found elsewhere that the color *can* enhance ad processing.

MARIO: I think this discussion underscores the importance of content, whether in prototypes or "real" newspapers. People usually read newspapers for specific purposes. They want sports scores, or they want to find out what happened in the Middle East last night. The nature of the content is the primary motivator, not the commercial messages, the size, or even the color.

PEGIE: I agree that content is the primary attraction for most readers. I think you could print "Dear Abby" upside-down with a purple screen over it and readers would still find it and read it.

MARIO: Exactly. Content is what I call the "ultimate tool" in our design process. The whole point of what we do in writing, editing, and design is to enhance the reader's ability to find and digest the information, whether that's hard news, features, recipes, or opinion columns. We must facilitate that process with our designs, and color is simply one of the tools. It's an important one, but only one.

ED: Nice speech. But did you learn everything about color you wanted to?

MARIO: No, not at all. One thing we have not tested for is "bad color." I sometimes hear criticism of our color research from people who say we test only with newspapers in St. Petersburg or other cities that print color well. We didn't test readers' reactions to bad color.

PEGIE: Good point, but would there be any difference?

MARIO: I'm not sure. We haven't tested for it and readers don't bring it up in their responses in the study. For example, look at the green helmet on the female soldier on the front page. In some sites the reproduction of that color was off a bit, at least by my standards. But the results didn't indicate that made any difference.

PEGIE: I hope we're not suggesting that it doesn't make any difference if color is less than the best.

ED: Let me up in the pulpit here, because my favorite sermon is that quality is important in everything, and that's particularly true when you're talking about color reproduction. In the introduction to the book, Mario points out that the readers of our future have been raised with television, and for the last 25 years or so that has meant color television. Readers are not only accustomed to color, they're accustomed to quality color—in television, magazines, billboards. Essentially every commercial message they receive, other than on radio, is in color. Think about it. Why would anyone buy a black-and-white television set these days? Color is fully integrated into the culture of communication, so if we use color poorly, readers know it.

MARIO: I agree with the point about color quality. We should not tolerate anything less than perfect reproduction. But on the other side of that, I think readers have a far higher tolerance for design and innovation than we give them credit for. And I see in this study a tolerance for brighter and stronger colors.

PEGIE: The study certainly shows that readers are not stuck in conventional patterns as they move around pages. All our age-old notions about lead positions and left-to-right eye movements are just that—notions. Readers seemed to be attracted to the dominant images, whether dominance was established by color, size, or positioning.

ED: They also have a tolerance for surprise. When Robert Lockwood designed all those wonderful pages in Allentown in the late 1970s and early 1980s, I never had readers ask me about page design, cvcn when an entire front page was a list of gas stations open during an energy crisis, or when half the front promoted good stories inside. Readers were far more flexible and responsive to innovation than we had dared dream. We were the ones mired in journal-ism's dogma. Readers simply responded to what worked.

PEGIE: Yes, and I think in this study we can see reader responses to various patterns of design. If we moved the strong color photograph, we could affect their reading patterns. When we grouped related photos, we found the processing was often enhanced. It seemed that they were saying, "Don't make us fumble around out here on a page. Give us some direction."

MARIO: I see it in terms of a dance performance. The audience doesn't see the rehearsals or the alternative choreography or the blistered feet. The audience sees only movement, light, emotion. I think we should choreograph the page for readers intelligently, making decisions for readers while offering choices, but taking charge of the process by not expecting the audience to choreograph the dance.

PEGIE: We usually call that editing.

ED: Exactly, but too many papers aren't "edited" in that sense. They follow formulas, AP budgets, or the editor's habits. Good design has to be focused on readers' needs and responses.

MARIO: In other words, too many of us in newspapers have a "stylebook" approach, whereas readers are far more flexible and tolerant.

ED: How cautious should we be, however, about drawing conclusions from this research?

SHARON: You must remember this study was designed to look only at color issues. You've come up with some remarkable correlations with other elements of design and content, but you have to be careful. Conceptually you are probably on the right track, but this prototype research may exaggerate certain findings that are not related to color, such as reading. For example, with fewer stories to look through and stories that were particularly well selected, written, and edited, readers seem to have spent more time than we typically see in a "real" newspaper.

ED: Are you saying the numbers are wrong?

SHARON: No, they are accurate, but before you can project the non-color findings to "real" newspapers, you need further research on these issues. In the meantime, you can use this research as a useful guide to reader behavior, but not as a rule book.

PEGIE: One thing we haven't talked about much is the role of television in all this. We still design newspapers as if television doesn't exist.

ED: Do you have some suggestions?

PEGIE: Yes. We should use newspapers as an expansion of what's on television. We can't scoop the competition anymore, but we can explain, amplify, and analyze. We still write long, boring stories conveying information that television dispatches in 60 seconds. We must go beyond all that.

ED: I'm smiling because I've been hearing this call to arms since 1960.

PEGIE: That's my point. The need for change has been obvious for a long time. But it must start with attitude. In Detroit, for example, we designed an Olympics package by recognizing that our readers were also viewers. What could we give our readers to use in conjunction with television? We didn't see the situation as a win-or-lose competition with television for the minds and hearts of readers. In the readers' minds, we were a partner in the process.

MARIO: To do this, however, we need to reconsider how we plan our work. I think one impact of this research will be to encourage newspapers to experiment with some different ways of managing the news operation. For example, I think we can see how much better it would be if one person designed facing pages. The rules we used to follow to design one page actually apply across two facing pages, so we should reorganize ourselves around that reality.

PEGIE: That's right, and this study might also pro-mote more extensive teamwork, which we so badly need in newsrooms.

DON: I agree. I also think these studies confirm some Poynter rhetoric about copy editors as the most important writers in the newspaper. Headlines and cutlines draw the readers to the lead of a story, so the people who write headlines and cutlines have to write them well, or the reader will never reach the golden prose.

MARIO: I think it goes back to the "WED" concepts we've been exploring at Poynter for several years.

ED: Explain that a bit more.

MARIO: At The Poynter Institute, we have tried to integrate our thinking and teaching of writing, editing, and design, what we call the "WED" concept, to try to show the connections, not just reinforce the divisions. Design is not just decoration or layout. The first real design steps are story assignments. Editing is a design function since it helps shape the final outcome. Page layout is only one component of design near the end of a longer process.

ED: What does this study tell you about the "WED" concept?

MARIO: It tells me that we're on the right track, that you can't separate the content from how you present it. Readers' movements around the page are governed by so many factors that the skills and tasks required to plan that journey for the readers must be highly integrated.

DON: Exactly so, and that integration of design can begin with reporters, who can be encouraged to write in modules or blocks instead of the hideous pyramid, to write "leadish" first paragraphs for each of the blocks, and to write their own subheads and even headlines.

ED: I hate to play the role of the history professor here, but I must remind you that's not the way most newspapers are organized. We segregate writers from photographers. We isolate copy editors from early decisions they ought to be a part of. We separate tasks that should be connected. We work in hierarchies of authority, not circles of interest.

MARIO: I know that all too well, but to get the kind of editing and planning that Pegie and I see as necessary to better written, edited, and designed newspapers, we need to convince editors of the need for more integrated organizations.

ED: Will this study help?

MARIO: I think so. For one thing it challenges many of our notions about how readers go through the newspaper. We can't talk about "lead" position anymore. The "lead" position is where inventive editors and designers choose to put it. We can see the power and limitations of

color in new ways. We see that black-and-white photography is not dead, that it still can have great impact and strength. We see that primary colors, bolder colors, are tolerated and perhaps even preferred by readers.

ED: Will it change how you design newspapers?

MARIO: It already has. I've begun to feel more confident about using stronger colors, about using color more aggressively. I don't mean "colorization." I do mean using color with more vigor to emphasize and organize the content.

ED: There's that word again—content. Let's get back to that as we try to wrap this up. As an editor, I seem to have a genetically inherited urge to get readers to read everything in the newspaper. Clearly they don't do that. How should we recast our intentions?

DON: We can start by not dividing everyone into two camps: "loyal readers" and "scanners." I think all readers, especially the good ones, are scanners.

PEGIE: I don't think it's realistic to expect readers to read everything, so I think the intention of the design must be to organize the traffic patterns so readers can get to the material they want or need that day, and to organize the specific information so it's first attractive and then comprehensible.

MARIO: I agree. I also think we need to recognize that "scanner" is not a dirty word. Don has pointed out that most of us are scanners. I'd like to add to that by reminding us that the "scanner" is probably our most intelligent reader. After all, the higher you went in your education, the more you had to learn how to scan vast amounts of material. So these are not lazy or illiterate people. Scanners are intelligent and experienced readers. Our task is to give them material that's worthy of their scan, that makes them stop scanning and start reading.

ED: I like that: Provide content worth stopping for and guide the reader toward it. Good advice to end our conversation.

Don Fry is director of the writing programs at The Poynter Institute. He is a former English professor and co-editor with Mario Garcia of *Color in American Newspapers*.

Mario Garcia directed The Poynter Institute graphics programs from 1982 to 1990. He has designed more than 100 newspapers around the world.

Edward D. Miller is an associate of The Poynter Institute and a former editor and publisher of *The Morning Call* in Allentown, Pennsylvania.

Sharon Polansky is vice president of Gallup Applied Science of Princeton, New Jersey. She directed the EYE-TRAC® Research for this study.

Pegie Stark is an associate professor at the University of Florida and a Poynter associate. Beginning in January 1991, she will direct the Institute's graphics programs.

STATISTICS

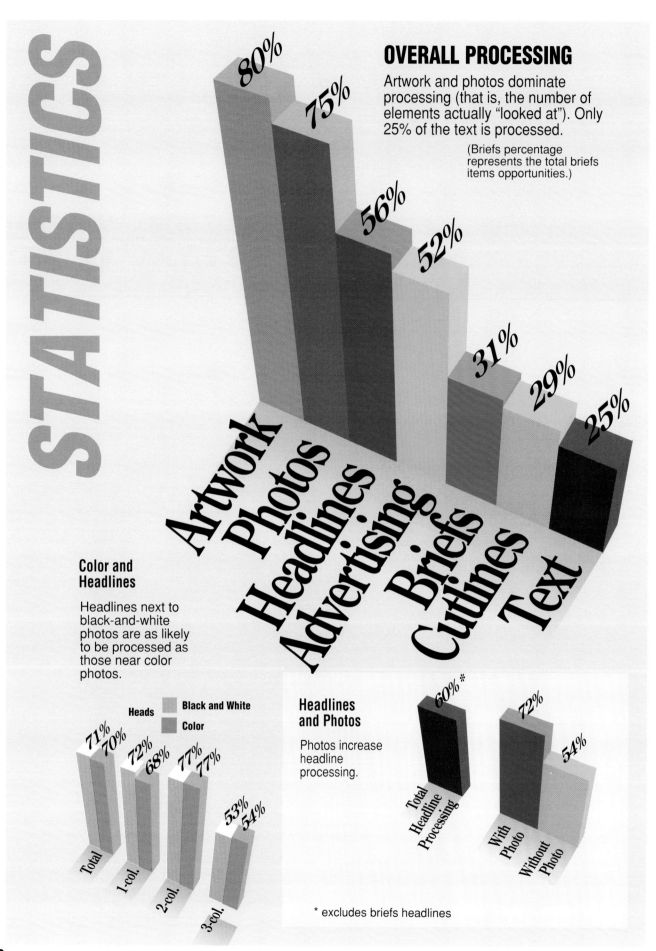

STATISTICS

OVERALL PROCESSING

Artwork and photos dominate processing (that is, the number of elements actually "looked at"). Only 25% of the text is processed.

(Briefs percentage represents the total briefs items opportunities.)

80%
75%
56%
52%
31%
29%
25%

Artwork
Photos
Headlines
Advertising
Briefs
Cutlines
Text

Color and Headlines

Headlines next to black-and-white photos are as likely to be processed as those near color photos.

Heads
Black and White
Color

71% 70%
72% 68%
77% 77%
53% 54%

Total
1-col.
2-col.
3-col.

Headlines and Photos

Photos increase headline processing.

60%*
72%
54%

Total Headline Processing
With Photo
Without Photo

* excludes briefs headlines

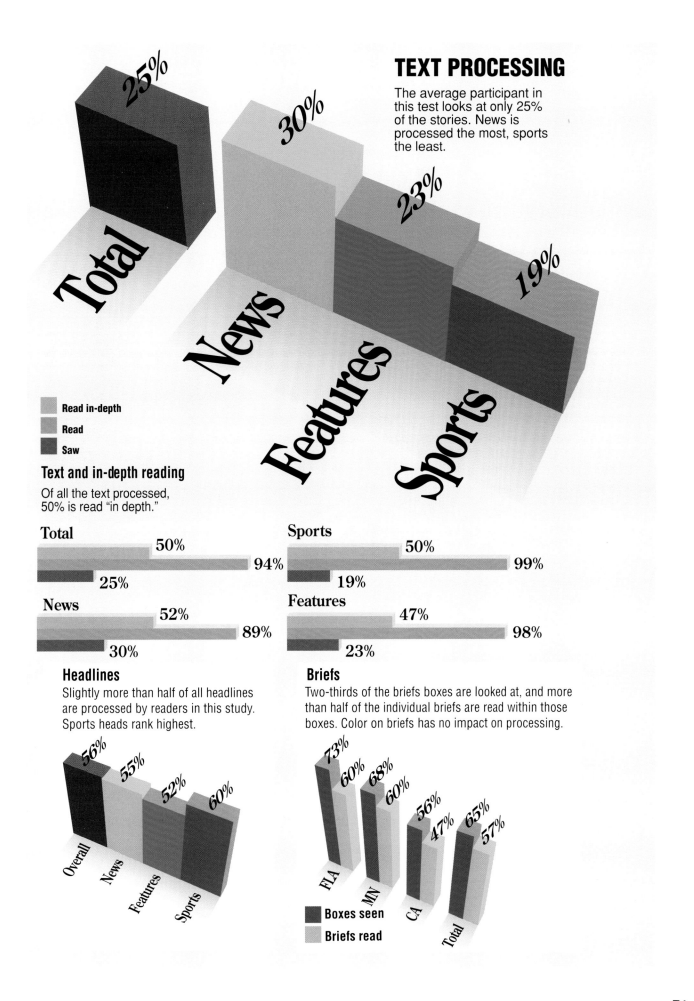

TEXT PROCESSING

The average participant in this test looks at only 25% of the stories. News is processed the most, sports the least.

25%

30%

23%

19%

Total

News

Features

Sports

- Read in-depth
- Read
- Saw

Text and in-depth reading

Of all the text processed, 50% is read "in depth."

Total
50%
94%
25%

News
52%
89%
30%

Sports
50%
99%
19%

Features
47%
98%
23%

Headlines

Slightly more than half of all headlines are processed by readers in this study. Sports heads rank highest.

56% 55% 52% 60%

Overall News Features Sports

Briefs

Two-thirds of the briefs boxes are looked at, and more than half of the individual briefs are read within those boxes. Color on briefs has no impact on processing.

73% 60% 68% 60% 56% 47% 65% 57%

FLA MN CA Total

- Boxes seen
- Briefs read

71

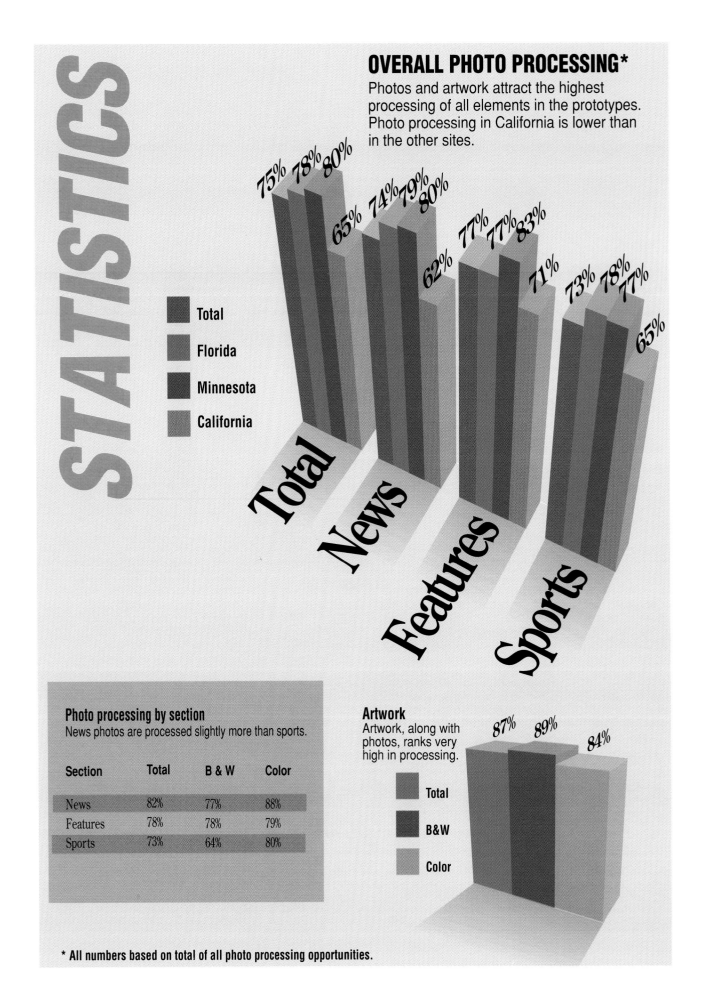

STATISTICS

OVERALL PHOTO PROCESSING*

Photos and artwork attract the highest processing of all elements in the prototypes. Photo processing in California is lower than in the other sites.

- Total
- Florida
- Minnesota
- California

Total: 75% 78% 80%

News: 65% 74% 79% 80%

Features: 62% 77% 77% 83%

Sports: 71% 73% 78% 77% 65%

Photo processing by section
News photos are processed slightly more than sports.

Section	Total	B & W	Color
News	82%	77%	88%
Features	78%	78%	79%
Sports	73%	64%	80%

Artwork
Artwork, along with photos, ranks very high in processing.

87% 89% 84%

- Total
- B&W
- Color

* All numbers based on total of all photo processing opportunities.

Photo groups processing

Color increases the chance for groups of photos to be seen, even when the photos are small.
(Photo group on page 13 of prototypes)

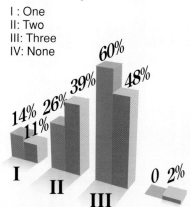

Prototype A (Color)
Prototype B (B&W)

Number of photos seen
I : One
II: Two
III: Three
IV: None

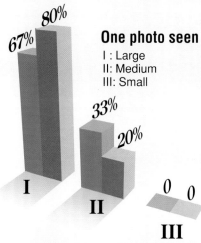

One photo seen
I : Large
II: Medium
III: Small

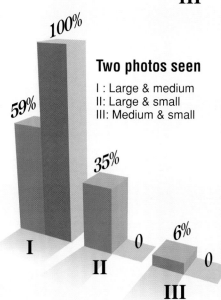

Two photos seen
I : Large & medium
II: Large & small
III: Medium & small

Photo processing and size

Size affects processing. The larger the photo, the more likely it is to be processed.

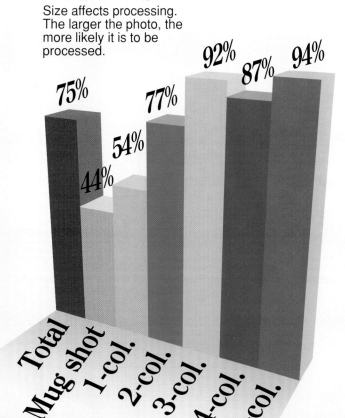

Cutline processing

Cutlines with color photos are processed slightly more than cutlines with black-and-white photos.

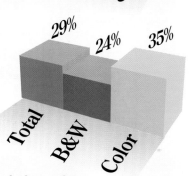

Cutline processing and photo size

Cutline reading increases with photo size.

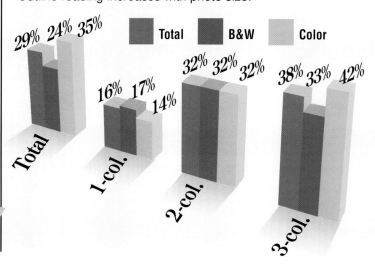

73

HOW MALES AND FEMALES PROCESS INFORMATION

In this study there is no significant difference in the ways males and females process elements in the newspaper. Here are the break-downs showing the slight differences in specific items processed.

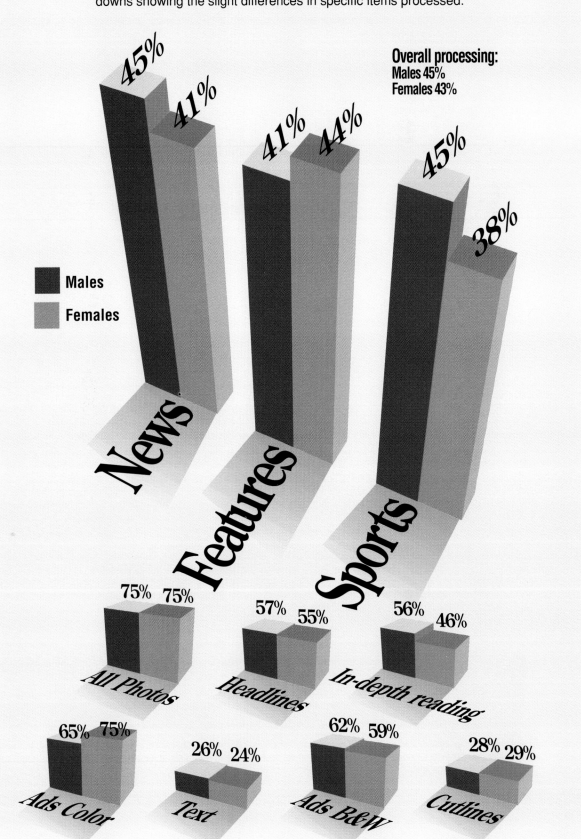

Overall processing:
Males 45%
Females 43%

Males

Females

45% 41% News
41% 44% Features
45% 38% Sports

75% 75% All Photos
57% 55% Headlines
56% 46% In-depth reading

65% 75% Ads Color
26% 24% Text
62% 59% Ads B&W
28% 29% Cutlines

If you would like to build on this research to improve your newspaper, consider this advice:

■ Accept these results as a starting point, not the final word. The numbers in the study are too small to draw certain kinds of conclusions.

■ Recognize the limits of the methodology. We set out to test only how readers process color.

—We did not test for reader comprehension. Nor would the prototype allow us to test for the effect of breaking news.

—Important unmeasured variables include such things as writing quality and photo composition.

—Readers were not tested in their normal reading environments, such as at the breakfast table, but in an unfamiliar room with the equipment on their heads.

With these important qualifications in mind, use the results to stimulate thinking, argument, innovation, and planning.

■ Pass this book around the newsroom to editors, designers, photographers, reporters, and others interested in the process. Begin conversations, perhaps at a brown-bag lunch, about how your paper uses color. Divide the group into teams and debate the research and its conclusions.

■ Look with special attention at the facts that contradict your assumptions about how readers see the page. Critique your paper in terms of the research results. Are you making decisions routinely and conventionally, without thinking of the consequences?

■ Make a list of your assumptions about how readers read. Now go down your list and ask yourself how you know that. Are you making important editorial decisions based on untested assumptions? How long has it been since you reviewed the "standard" list of colors that you use on your front page?

■ Discuss the decision-making processes at your newspaper. What contributes to collaborative relationships in the newsroom? What inhibits them? How might you change that for the better?

■ Make believe you are starting a new newspaper in your town. You will have the capability to use a great deal of color. Based on this research and your own experience, design a work environment that will let you make best use of this important tool.

So begin talking to each other in the newsroom. Call or write us at The Poynter Institute to share your reactions to this research. And remember: The journey is as important as the destination.

THE LAST WORD

BIBLIOGRAPHY

COLOR IN NEWSPAPERS: A SELECTED BIBLIOGRAPHY

By Jo Cates, Chief Librarian
The Poynter Institute for Media Studies

This bibliography contains selected books and articles on the use of color in newspapers, picking up from the bibliography in *Color in American Newspapers* (The Poynter Institute for Media Studies, 1986) and including items published through July 1990. In addition, it includes some earlier materials omitted from the first color bibliography.

I. Books and Annual Publications

Albers, Josef. *Interaction of Color.* Text of the original edition with revised plate section. Rev. pocket ed. New Haven: Yale University Press, 1975.

Allen, Jeanne. *Designer's Guide to Color 3.* San Francisco: Chronicle Books, 1986.

Birren, Faber. *Color and Human Response.* New York: Van Nostrand Reinhold, 1978. (Birren is also the author of *Light, Color and Environment,* Van Nostrand Reinhold, 1969, and *Color Psychology and Color Therapy*, Citadel Press, 1984.)

Bruno, Michael H. *Principles of Color Proofing: A Manual on the Measurement and Control of Tone and Color Reproduction.* Salem, NH: Gama Communications, 1986.

Buckley, Mary. *Color Theory: A Guide to Information Sources.* Detroit: Gale, 1975.

Chevreul, M.E. *The Principles of Harmony and Contrast of Color.* New York: Van Nostrand Reinhold, 1981. (Originally published in France in 1839 as *La loi du contraste simultané des couleurs.*)

Chijiiwa, Hideaki. *Color Harmony: A Guide to Creative Color Combinations.* Tr. by Keiki Nakamura. Rockport, MA: Rockport Pub., 1986.

Color and the Computer. H. John Durrett, ed. Boston: Academic Press, 1987.

Color in American Newspapers. Mario R. Garcia and Don Fry, eds. St. Petersburg, FL: The Poynter Institute for Media Studies, 1986.

Color Proofing 1980-1985: A Selected Bibliography. Allen Ko, comp. Richard Schmidle, ed. Rochester, NY: Rochester Institute of Technology, 1986.

Color Scanners 1984-1985: A Selected Bibliography. Phil Winter, comp. Richard Schmidle, ed. Rochester, NY: Rochester Institute of Technology, 1986.

The Color Symposium: Proceedings of a Poynter Institute for Media Studies Graphics and Design Seminar. St. Petersburg, FL: The Poynter Institute for Media Studies, 1985.

Current, Ira B. *Photographic Color Printing: Theory and Technique.* Boston: Focal Press, 1987.

De Grandis, Luigina. *Theory and the Use of Color.* Tr. by John Gilbert. New York: Abrams, 1986. (Translation of *Teoria e Uso del Colore.*)

Designer's Guide to Color 1, 2, 3. San Francisco: Chronicle Books, 1984.

Favre, Jean-Paul, and Andre November. *Color and Communication.* Zurich: ABC Verlag, 1979.

Garcia, Mario R. *Newspaper Colour Design.* Darmstadt, West Germany: The International Association for Newspaper and Media Technology (IFRA), 1989.

Gerstner, Karl. *The Forms of Color: The Interaction of Visual Elements.* Tr. by Dennis A. Stephenson. Cambridge, MA: MIT Press, 1986. (Translation of *Die Formen der Farben.*)

Hardin, C.L. *Color for Philosophers: Unweaving the Rainbow.* Indianapolis: Hackett Pub. Co., 1988.

Hirsch, Robert. *Exploring Color Photography.* Dubuque, IA: W.C. Brown, 1989.

Hunt, R.W.G. *The Reproduction of Colour: In Photography, Printing and Television.* 4th ed. Tolworth, England: Fountain Press, 1987.

Itten, Johannes. *The Color Star.* New York: Van Nostrand Reinhold, 1985. (Itten is also the author of *The Elements of Color*, Van Nostrand Reinhold, 1970; based on his book *The Art of Color*, published in Germany in 1961 under the title *Kunst der Farbe.*)

Ladau, Robert F., Brent K. Smith, and Jennifer Place. *Color in Interior Design and Architecture.* New York: Van Nostrand Reinhold, 1989.

Landesman, Charles. *Color and Consciousness: An Essay in Metaphysics.* Philadelphia: Temple University Press, 1989.

Marvullo, Joe. *Color Vision.* New York: AMPHOTO, 1989.

Marx, Ellen. *Optical Color & Simultaneity.* Tr. by Geoffrey O'Brien. New York: Van Nostrand Reinhold, 1983. (Translation of *Couleur Optique.* Includes transparencies.)

Newton, Isaac, Sir. *Opticks.* New York: Dover, 1952. (Originally published in 1704, London, by S. Smith and B. Walford.)

Sargent, Walter. *The Enjoyment and Use of Color.* New York: Dover Publications, 1964. ("Corrected and revised republication of work published in 1923.")

Satterwhite, Joy, and Al Satterwhite. *Satterwhite on Color and Design.* New York: AMPHOTO, 1986.

Southworth, Miles, and Donna Southworth. *Glossary of Color Scanner, Color System, and Communication Terms.* Livonia, NY: Graphic Arts Publishing Co., 1987.

A White Paper on Newspaper Color: A Special Report Published by the NPPA. George Sweers, ed. Designed by Pegie Stark. National Press Photographers Association, 1985.

II. Magazine, Periodical, and Newspaper Articles

Altman, Jennifer. "Scanner Reveals Brain's Colour Processor." *New Scientist,* 26 Aug. 1989, p. 30.

Anthony, Jay. "Printing Better Color Pictures." *Design,* 1985 Year-End Issue, p. 6.

Baugsto, Per H. "Norwegian Color." *Design,* v. 31, Sept. 1988, pp. 56-61.

Bellew, Bonnie, and Jeff Magness. "Color Track Focuses on Ethics and Quality." *Design,* v. 35, Dec. 1989, pp. A7-A8.

Bieberle, Gordon. "Color in Magazines." *Magazine Design and Production,* March 1989, pp. 60-67.

Bogart, Leo, and B. Stuart Tolley. "The Search for Information in Newspaper Advertising." *Journal of Advertising Research,* April-May 1988, pp. 9+. (Scanning and eye-tracking).

Bohle, Robert H. "Readers Tell Us About Color." *Design,* v. 21, 1986, pp. 8-15.

—. "The Value of Color in Newspaper Design." *Community College Journalist,* Summer 1987, pp. 10-12.

Bohle, Robert H., and Mario R. Garcia. "Reader Response to Color Halftones and Spot Color in Newspaper Design." *Journalism Quarterly* 64 (1987): 731-739.

Boynton, Robert M. "Color Vision." *Annual Review of Psychology* 39 (1988): 69-199.

Brou, Philippe, Thomas R. Sciascia, Lynette Linden, and Jerome Y. Lettvin. "The Color of Things." *Scientific American,* Sept. 1986, pp. 84+.

Chung, Robert Y., and Richard M. Adams, II. "Color Proofs: All Roles for All Players." *Magazine Design and Production,* Aug. 1989, pp. 50-54, 84.

"Color in Newspapers." *Editor & Publisher,* 24 Sept. 1988, pp. 1C-40C.

"Color in Newspapers." *Editor & Publisher,* 30 Sept. 1989, pp. 1C-32C.

"Color Section." *Editor & Publisher,* 26 Sept. 1987, pp. 1C-28C.

Covert, Douglas C. "Color Preference Conflicts in Visual Compositions." *Newspaper Research Journal* 9 (Fall 1987): 49-59.

Cunningham, H. Wilson. "ANPA/Color Standards Help Ensure That Colors Are Printed Accurately and Consistently." *presstime,* May 1989, pp. 100-102.

Curtis, Cathy. "Papers Learn to Fight Color With Color." *Advertising Age*, 20 July 1987, pp. S10-S13.

"Dogs Found to Recognize Some Colors in a Study." *The New York Times*, 26 Dec. 1989, p. B10. (See also "Orange You Glad? Fido Sees the Blues," in *Science News*, 30 Sept. 1989, p. 215.)

Gersh, Debra. "*New York Times* Gets Colorful with New TV Section." *Editor & Publisher,* 20 Feb. 1988, p. 17.

Gill, Tim. "The Color Era." *Magazine Design and Production*, March 1989, pp. 32-34.

Goetz, Jill. "Extra! Extra! Red All About It!" *Psychology Today*, July 1987, p. 24.

Goltz, Gene. "The Eyes Have It." *presstime,* Sept. 1987, pp. 14-15. (Gallup's EYE-TRAC® Research.)

Hoenig, Gary. "Low-Cost Scanners Offer the Razzle Without the Dazzle." *NewsInc.*, July/Aug. 1989, pp. 47, 50.

Hunter, Margaret. "Drupa (Druck und Papier) 90 Report: The Big News Was Color: Faster, Less Costly and Better." *Folio: The Magazine for Magazine Management*, July 1990, pp. 69-70, 73.

Jameson, Dorothea. "Some Misunderstandings About Color Perception, Color Mixture and Color Measurement." *Leonardo* 16 (Winter 1983): 41-42.

Kenney, Keith, and Stephen Lacy. "Economic Forces Behind Newspapers' Increasing Use of Color and Graphics." *Newspaper Research Journal* 8 (Spring 1987): 33-41.

Kinsolving, Charles, Jr. "Should We Make Color User-Friendly?" *Editor & Publisher,* 1 Oct. 1988, pp. 68, 50.

Leonard, Richard. "Quality Color—Controlling the Things That Money Can't Buy." *NewsInc.* Nov./Dec. 1989, pp. 47-50.

Levy, Bernard I. "Research Into the Psychological Meaning of Color." *American Journal of Art Therapy* 23 (1984): 58-62.

MacDonald, Stephen. "Eye-Stopping Design in the Supermarket." *The Wall Street Journal,* 22 Jan. 1988, p. 29. (Eye-tracking research.)

Murch, Gerald M., and Joann M. Taylor. "Sensible Color: A Human-Oriented System Makes Matching Screen and Hard-Copy Colors Easier." *Computer Graphics World,* July 1988, pp. 69-71.

Olsen, Gary. "Magic or Simple Tool: Color on the Mac." *Pre-,* July 1990, pp. 16-19.

Ostendorf, Bill. "Is Color Really Worth It?" *Design,* 1985 Year-End Issue, pp. 4-5.

Powers, Jack. "Desktop Color by the Numbers." *Folio: The Magazine for Magazine Management,* Feb. 1990, pp. 69-75.

—. "Desktop Color: Looking Better and Better." *Folio: The Magazine for Magazine Management.* March 1989, pp. 116-122.

Reveaux, Tony. "A Mac of Many Colors." *MacUser,* Jan. 1989, pp. 96+.

Rorick, George. "Color Separations with the Mac and New MacDraw II." *Design,* v. 27, March 1988, pp. 24-25.

Rosenberg, Jim. "Color Scanners." *Editor & Publisher,* 10 June 1989, pp. 88, 92, 94.

—. "High-Volume Offset Color for the 90s." *Editor & Publisher,* 4 March 1989, pp. 34-39.

—. "More Color for the Monitor." *Editor & Publisher,* 4 Feb. 1989, pp. 30-31. (*"Christian Science Monitor* redesigns after purchasing $1.8 million electronic color prepress and communications equipment from Scitex.")

Saleski, Charles G. "Standards for Color Viewing." *Magazine Design and Production,* July 1989, pp. 32, 35.

"Search for Color Pagination System Pays Off." *Pre-,* April 1989, p. 30.

Sellin, Karen Moody. "Macintosh Color Displays." *Computer Graphics World,* Nov. 1989, pp. 69-76.

Smith, Ron F. "How Design & Color Affect Reader Judgment of Newspapers." *Newspaper Research Journal* 10 (Winter 1989): 75-85.

Standen, Craig C. "What Makes a Newspaper Advertisement Effective? Large Illustrations, Color, Headlines and Style." *presstime,* July 1989, p. 72.

Stanton, Anthony P. "Controlling Color Reproduction in Newspapers." *GATFWORLD,* Jan./Feb. 1989, pp. 33-38.

Steffans, Brian. "How-To Tips on Color Graphics." *Design,* 1985 Year-End Issue, p. 7.

Terrell, Pamela M. "Art." *presstime,* Feb. 1989, pp. 20-27. ("Newspapers' historically gray pages have come alive with an explosion of color and graphics, many of them computer-assisted.")

Truitt, Rosalind C. "Color: How Good Can It Get?" *presstime,* May 1989, pp. 20-24.

Utt, Sandra H., and Steve Pasternack. "How They Look: An Updated Study of American Newspaper Front Pages." *Journalism Quarterly* 66 (Autumn 1989): 621-628.

—. "Subject Perception of Newspaper Characteristics Based on Front Page Design." *Newspaper Research Journal* 8 (1986): 29-35.

Virkus, Robert. "Desktop Links Are Changing the Color Market." *Folio: The Magazine for Magazine Management,* Nov. 1989, pp. 134-137.

—. "The Year of Color." *Pre-,* May 1990, pp. 26-29.

Young, Elliot. "Visibility Achieved by Outdoor Advertising." *Journal of Advertising Research*, Aug.-Sept. 1984, pp. 19-21. (Eye-tracking and outdoor advertisement boards.)

III. Studies, Reports, and Dissertations

Bohle, Robert H., and Mario R. Garcia. "Reader Reactions to Color in Newspapers." Paper presented at the annual meeting of the Association for Education in Journalism and Mass Communication, Norman, OK, Aug. 1986, ERIC ED 270802. 23 pp.

Gilbert, Kathy, and Joan Schleuder. "Effects of Color Complexity in Still Photographs on Mental Effort and Memory." Paper presented at the annual meeting of the Association for Education in Journalism and Mass Communication, Portland, OR, July 1988, ERIC ED 298579. 22 pp.

Lamberski, Richard J. "A Comprehensive and Critical Review of the Methodology and Findings in Color Investigations." Paper presented at the annual convention of the Association for Educational Communications and Technology, Denver, CO, April 1980, ERIC ED 194063. 44 pp.

Low, Jean Irene. "A Study of the Importance of Selected Graphic Procedures Used in Print Information for Adult Readers." M.A. thesis, University of Minnesota, 1989.

Pritchett, Thomas K. "An Experimental Test of the Impact of Color Environment on the Effectiveness of Color as an Attention-Producing Device in Magazine Advertising." Ph.D. dissertation, Florida State University, 1982.

Mario R. Garcia

Mario R. Garcia is an associate of The Poynter Institute for Media Studies in St. Petersburg, Florida, where he served as director of its graphics programs from 1982 to 1990. He is also a professor of mass communications at the University of South Florida and is visiting professor of graphic arts at Syracuse University's Newhouse School of Public Communications, whose faculty he joined in 1976. He is a regular workshop instructor at the IFRA Institute in West Germany as well as at seminars of the American Press Institute, where he has been a seminar leader since 1978.

Dr. Garcia is a design consultant to more than 100 newspapers across the United States, Canada, South America, Europe, and Asia.

He is the author of *Newspaper Colour Design*, published by IFRA in four languages in 1989; *Contemporary Newspaper Design: A Structural Approach* (Prentice-Hall, second edition 1987); co-author with Don Fry of *Color In American Newspapers* (The Poynter Institute for Media Studies, 1986); and co-author with Ben Blank of *Professional*

Video Graphic Design (Prentice-Hall, 1986). A Spanish version of *Contemporary Newspaper Design* was published in 1984 by EUNSA Press (Pamplona, Spain), under the title *Diseno y Remodelacion de Diarios*. Dr. Garcia is the author of numerous articles about newspaper design, and has been actively involved with *ANPA News Research Reports* about the impact of design on readers. His earlier publications include *The New Adviser: Learning the Craft* (Columbia Scholastic Press, 1974), a handbook for student publication advisers; and *The Student Newspaper Designer* (University of Oklahoma Scholastic Press, 1981).

Born in Cuba, he came to the United States at age 14. He received a bachelor's degree from the University of South Florida (1969), and his master of arts (1972) and doctorate (1976) from the University of Miami.

Dr. Garcia received a Lifetime Achievement Award for services to the school press and journalism education from the University of Oklahoma's H.H. Herbert School of Journalism and Mass Communications, and was installed in the school's Scholastic Journalism Hall of Fame. Garcia was also installed in the Florida Community College Advisers Association's Hall of Fame in 1984, and was awarded the Gold Key from Columbia University Scholastic Press Association in 1981 for services to the teaching of journalism.

His design awards include a Silver Award from the Society of Newspaper Design (SND) for his 1985 redesign of *Novedades* in Mexico City (in collaboration with Roger Black), plus a Distinguished Award of Merit from the Mexican Academy of Design for his work on *Novedades.* In addition, he has received SND awards for the redesigns of *The Messenger-Inquirer* (1984), *Novedades* (1985), *The Daily Breeze* (1986), *El Nuevo Herald* (1987), *The New Paper* (1988), *Arhus Stiftstidende* (1989), and *El Comercio*'s Economic Section (1989).

Pegie Stark

Pegie Stark, an associate of The Poynter Institute for Media Studies, is an associate professor at the University of Florida, where she has taught informational graphics and newspaper design for two years. Beginning in January 1991, she will direct the graphics and design programs at The Poynter Institute.

Dr. Stark has served as graphics editor at the *Detroit News*, graphics director at *The Detroit Free Press*, and art editor at the *St. Petersburg Times*.

She is international chair for the Society of Newspaper Design (SND) and writes articles for *Design,* the SND journal.

She has been a lecturer on newspaper design and informational graphics at the American Press Institute,

IFRA Research Association, SND/Scandinavia, Association for Education in Journalism and Mass Communications, the Southern Newspaper Publishers Association, and various universities and newspaper societies.

Dr. Stark received a master's degree and doctorate in mass communications from Indiana University. Her dissertation was a survey of 112 front-page editors addressing issues of newspaper design principles and practices. While working on her master's and doctorate at Indiana University, she taught photography and newspaper

design. Previously she had taught lithography, painting, and photography at the Indianapolis Museum of Art, the Indianapolis Art League, and the John Herron School of Art in Indianapolis.

She received a bachelor's degree in fine arts with distinction from the John Herron School of Art. After graduation she operated a lithographic print shop specializing in limited editions for local artists. Her work has been exhibited in Indiana and Arizona.

She has received SND awards for art directing, research, and editing of informational graphics, and has been the recipient of research awards from The Poynter Institute, Scripps-Howard Foundation, and Indiana University. While at Indiana University she received the Lieber Teaching Award (1984).

Mario Garcia and Pegie Stark assemble visual notes, art, and pages for *Eyes on the News* at The Poynter Institute, summer 1990.

The text and graphics for this book were created, designed, and produced electronically on Macintosh™ computers.

The original text was created in Microsoft Word®. Preliminary page designs were created in QuarkXPress™, then faxed back and forth as the authors traveled the world on design projects. Original text, edited copy, information and text for graphics, graphic proofs, and final versions were sent via PressLink™ and fax to various writers, editors, and artists across the United States working on specific sections.

Chart information was plotted in DeltaGraph™ (DeltaPoint). Graphics and illustrations were drawn using MacDraw II® (Claris), Illustrator® (Adobe), and FreeHand® (Aldus). Canvas Separator® (Deneba) was used to convert Quickdraw graphics to EPS format. Artwork was finalized in FreeHand®. All text and graphics were imported into QuarkXPress 3.0™ for final layout and design. Full pages with color separations for graphics and illustrations were printed out from a Linotronic™ typesetter. Color photos were produced by traditional color separation methods.

Body text typeface: Century Oldstyle

Headline typeface: Helvetica Condensed Bold

Chapter heads and labels: Helvetica Condensed Black

Text for informational graphics: Helvetica and Helvetica Condensed